Engaging God's Word

Ephesians

Engage Bible Studies

Tools That Transform

Engage Bible Studies

an imprint of

 COMMUNITY BIBLE STUDY

Engaging God's Word: Ephesians
Copyright © 2012 by Community Bible Study. All rights reserved.
ISBN 978-1-62194-003-6

Published by Community Bible Study
790 Stout Road
Colorado Springs, CO
1-800-826-4181
www.communitybiblestudy.org

Printed in the United States of America.

Contents

Introduction 5
    Why Study the Bible? 5
    How to Get the Most out of *Engaging God's Word* 7

Lesson 1   All Things Are United in Christ 11

Lesson 2   Hope for the Hopeless (Ephesians 1:1-14) 17

Lesson 3   To Know the God Who First Knew Us
                (Ephesians 1:15-23) 25

Lesson 4   The Key to Salvation (Ephesians 2:1-10) 33

Lesson 5   Christ the Bridge Builder (Ephesians 2:11-22) 41

Lesson 6   Paul and His Ministry (Ephesians 3:1-13) 49

Lesson 7   The Power and the Glory (Ephesians 3:14-21) 57

Lesson 8   Growing Into the Likeness of Christ (Ephesians 4:1-16) . . 65

Lesson 9   Put off the Old Self, Put on the New (Ephesians 4:17-32) . . . 73

Lesson 10 The Imitation of Christ (Ephesians 5:1-20) 81

Lesson 11 Divine Rules for Human Relationships
                (Ephesians 5:21–6:9) 89

Lesson 12 The Armor of God (Ephesians 6:10-24) 97

Small Group Leader's Guide 105

About Community Bible Study 108

Introduction

Welcome to the life-changing adventure of engaging with God's Word!
Whether this is the first time you've opened a Bible or you've studied
the Scriptures all your life, good things are in store for you. Studying
the Bible is unlike any other kind of study you have ever done. That's
because the Word of God is *"living and active"* (Hebrews 4:12) and
transcends time and cultures. The earth and heavens as we know them
will one day pass away, but God's Word never will (Mark 13:31). It's
as relevant to your life today as it was to the people who wrote it down
centuries ago. And the fact that God's Word is living and active means
that reading God's Word is always meant to be a personal experience.
God's Word is not just dead words on a page—it is page after page
of living, powerful words—so get ready, because the time you spend
studying the Bible in this *Engaging God's Word* course will be life-
transforming!

Why Study the Bible?

Some Christians read the Bible because they know they're supposed to.
It's a good thing to do, and God expects it. And all that's true! However,
there are many additional reasons to study God's Word. Here are just
some of them.

We get to know God through His Word. Our God is a relational God
who knows us and wants us to know Him. The Scriptures, which He
authored, reveal much about Him: how He thinks and feels, what His
purposes are, what He thinks about us, how He views the world He
made, what He has planned for the future. The Bible shows us God's
many attributes—His kindness, goodness, justice, love, faithfulness,
mercy, compassion, creativity, redemption, sovereignty, and so on. As
we get to know Him through His Word, we come to love and trust Him.

God speaks to us through His Word. One of the primary ways God speaks to us is through His written Word. Don't be surprised if, as you read the Bible, certain parts nearly jump off the page at you, almost as if they'd been written with you in mind. God is the Author of this incredible book, so that's not just possible, it's likely! Whether it is to find comfort, warning, correction, teaching, or guidance, always approach God's Word with your spiritual ears open (Isaiah 55:3) because God, your loving heavenly Father, has things He wants to say to you.

God's Word brings life. Just about everyone wants to learn the secret to "the good life." And the good news is, that secret is found in God's Word. Don't think of the Bible as a bunch of rules. Viewing it with that mindset is a distortion. God gave us His Word because as our Creator and the Creator of the universe, He alone knows how life was meant to work. He knows that love makes us happier than hate, that generosity brings more joy than greed, and that integrity allows us to rest more peacefully at night than deception does. God's ways are not always "easiest" but they are the way to life. As the Psalmist says, *"If Your law had not been my delight, I would have perished in my affliction. I will never forget Your precepts, for by them You have given me life"* (Psalm 119:92-93).

God's Word offers stability in an unstable world. Truth is an ever-changing negotiable for many people in our culture today. But building your life on constantly changing "truth" is like building your house on shifting sand. God's Word, like God Himself, never changes. What He says was true yesterday, is true today, and will still be true a billion years from now. Jesus said, *"Everyone then who hears these words of Mine and does them will be like a wise man who built his house on the rock"* (Matthew 7:24).

God's Word helps us to pray effectively. When we read God's Word and get to know what He is really like, we understand better how to pray. God answers prayers that are according to His will. We discover His will by reading the Bible. First John 5:14-15 tells us that *"this is the confidence that we have toward Him, that if we ask anything according to His will He hears us. And if we know that He hears us in whatever we ask, we know that we have the requests that we have asked of Him."*

How to Get the Most out of *Engaging God's Word*

Each *Engaging God's Word* study contains key elements that have been carefully designed to help you get the most out of your time in God's Word. Slightly modified for your study-at-home success, this approach is very similar to the tried-and-proven Bible study method that Community Bible Study has used with thousands of men, women, and children across the United States and around the world for nearly 40 years. There are some basic things you can expect to find in each course in this series.

❖ Lesson 1 provides an overview of the Bible book (or books) you will study and questions to help you focus, anticipate, and pray about what you will be learning.

❖ Every lesson contains questions to answer on your own, commentary that reviews and clarifies the passage, and three special sections called "Apply what you have learned," "Think about" and "Personalize this lesson."

❖ Some lessons contain memory verse suggestions.

Whether you plan to use *Engaging God's Word* on your own or with a group, here are some suggestions that will help you enjoy and receive the most benefit from your study.

Spread out each lesson over several days. Your *Engaging God's Word* lessons were designed to take a week to complete. Spreading out your study rather than doing it all at once allows time for the things God is teaching you to sink in and for you to practice applying them.

Pray each time you read God's Word. The Bible is a book unlike any other because God Himself inspired it. The same Spirit who inspired the human authors who wrote it will help you to understand and apply it if you ask Him to. So make it a practice to ask Him to make His Word come alive to you every time you read it.

Read the whole passage covered in the lesson. Before plunging into the questions, take time to read the specific chapter or verses that will be covered in that lesson. Doing this will give you important context for the whole lesson. Reading the Bible in context is an important principle in interpreting it accurately.

Begin learning the memory verse. Learning Scripture by heart requires discipline, but the rewards far outweigh the effort. Memorizing a verse allows you to recall it whenever you need it—for personal encouragement and direction, or to share with someone else. Consider writing the verse on a sticky note or index card that you can post where you will see it often or carry with you to review during the day. Reading and re-reading the verse often—out loud when possible—is a simple way to commit it to memory.

Re-read the passage for each section of questions. Each lesson is divided into sections so that you study one small part of Scripture at a time. Before attempting to answer the questions, review the verses that the questions will cover.

Answer the questions without consulting the Commentary or other reference materials. There is great joy in having the Holy Spirit teach you God's Word on your own, without the help of outside resources. Don't cheat yourself of the delight of discovery by reading the Commentary prematurely. Wait until after you've completed the lesson.

Repeat the process for all the question sections.

Prayerfully consider the "Apply what you have learned," marked with the 📌 push pin symbol. The vision of Community Bible Study is not to just gain knowledge about the Bible, but to be transformed by it. For this reason, each set of questions closes with a section that encourages you to apply what you are learning. Usually this section involves action—something for you to do. As you practice these suggestions, your life will change.

Read the Commentary. *Engaging God's Word* commentaries are written by theologians whose goal is to help you understand the context of what you are studying as it relates to the rest of Scripture, God's character, and what the passage means for your life. Of necessity, the commentaries include the author's interpretations. While interesting and helpful, keep in mind that the Commentary is simply one person's understanding of what these passages mean. Other godly men and women have views that are also worth considering.

Pause to contemplate each "Think about" section, marked with the notepad symbol. These features, embedded in the Commentary, offer a place to pause and consider some of the principles being brought out by the text. They provide excellent ideas to journal about or to discuss with other believers, especially those doing the study with you.

Jot down insights or prayer points from the "Personalize this lesson" marked with the ☑ check box symbol. While the "Apply what you have learned" section focuses on doing, the "Personalize this lesson" section focuses on becoming. Spiritual transformation is not just about doing right things and refraining from doing wrong things—it is about changing from the inside out. To be transformed means letting God change our hearts so that our attitudes, emotions, desires, reactions, and goals are increasingly like Jesus'. Often this section will discuss something that you cannot do in your own strength—so your response will usually be something to pray about. Remember that becoming more Christ-like is not just a matter of trying harder—it requires God's empowerment.

Lesson 1

All Things Are United in Christ

The apostle Paul's letters to churches often followed this outline: *Christ has saved you and given you a whole new life, which includes these benefits.... Now, here's what your new Christian life should look like in practical terms....* This pattern is seen more clearly in Ephesians than any of Paul's other letters.

The first three chapters:

❖ Paul emphasizes Christ's eternality (1:5-6); His work of redemption (1:7-9); His supremacy (1:19-22); His grace (2:5, 8); His ministry of reconciliation (2:11-19); His personal sacrifice (2:13); His centrality to the church (2:19-22); His riches (3:8); His role as the Agent of God's purpose (3:11); His role as Mediator (3:12); and His being the Recipient of glory (3:21).

❖ Because of Christ's sacrifice, four times Paul refers to believers being in or having access to *"heavenly places."*

❖ Paul emphasizes that, together, these individual believers (regardless of their ethnic origin) who are in *"heavenly places"* make up one body—the church.

The final three chapters:

❖ Paul explains how believers should respond to the truths he expounded on in the first three chapters. These chapters are full of verbs: *"I ... urge;" "you must;" "put off;" "speak the truth;" "Let no;" "do not;" "Let all;"* and the list goes on....

❖ A verb he repeats throughout this section is *"walk"* (five times), referring to ongoing behavior.

❖   Paul emphasizes that, individually and corporately, believers need
    to live (*"walk"*) in the full power of the Holy Spirit so that when
    the world sees the diverse members of the church it sees One—
    Christ.

1. Why do you think Paul emphasized Christ's work before
    advising the believers about their lifestyle choices?

    _____

    _____

    _____

2. What do you think Paul meant when he referred to *"heavenly
    places"*?

    _____

    _____

    _____

3. What does it mean to you to be a member of Christ's body?

    _____

    _____

    _____

    _____

*If you are doing this study with a group, take time to pray for one another
about your answers to question 3. Ask God to show you the depth of joy found
in being a member of Christ's body. If you are studying by yourself, write your
prayer in the blank space below.*

All Things Are United in Christ

The letter to the Ephesians was written to 1st-century Christians in and around Ephesus to tell them about God's eternal plan and purpose for His church. Through the centuries, it has encouraged understanding of deep spiritual truth. It also seeks to activate the will so that daily life and practice of faith will be aligned with God's eternal plan. Paul strives to describe the enthroned Christ who is Lord of the church, the world, and the entire created order. As the ascended Lord, Jesus Christ is completing the work He began in His earthly ministry by means of His "extended body," the church. God's goal is to fill all things with Christ and bring all things to Christ.

What Do We Know About Ephesus?

In Paul's day, Ephesus was a large and important city on the west coast of the Roman province of Asia (modern Turkey). Situated at the mouth of the Cayster River, Ephesus was the most favorable seaport in the province of Asia and the most important trade center west of Tarsus, Paul's birthplace. Although Pergamum was the capital of Roman Asia, Ephesus, with a population of perhaps 300,000, was the largest city in the province.

Another factor in Ephesus' prominence was religion. The temple to Artemis (also known by her Roman name, Diana) ranked as one of the seven wonders of the ancient world. Artemis was known variously as the moon goddess, the goddess of the hunt, and the patroness of young girls. The temple at Ephesus housed her multi-breasted image, which was reputed to have fallen from heaven. During the Roman period, coins were minted with the inscription "Diana of Ephesus."

Christianity first came to Ephesus in the middle of the 1ˢᵗ century, perhaps as a result of the efforts of Priscilla and Aquila (see Acts 18), or perhaps arising from the large colony of Jews there. Paul came to Ephesus in about AD 52 and established a resident ministry there for the better part of three years, during which time he wrote 1 Corinthians. He taught during the hot midday hours in the lecture hall of a certain Tyrannus and, because Ephesus was a crossroads city, the word spread. Luke reports that *"all the residents of Asia heard the word of the Lord, both Jews and Greeks"* (Acts 19:10).

Paul's influence in Ephesus angered the silversmiths' league, which made souvenirs of the temple. They feared that the preaching of the gospel would undermine their lucrative business. As a result, a silversmith named Demetrius incited a riot against Paul.

When Paul departed from Ephesus, he left Timothy to combat false teaching. Christian tradition is unanimous that the apostle John resided in Ephesus toward the end of the 1ˢᵗ century. In his vision from the island of Patmos off the coast of Asia Minor, John describes Ephesus as a flourishing though complacent church beset with false teachers and having lost its first love. Ephesus continued to play a prominent role in early church history. A long line of Eastern bishops resided there, and in AD 431, the Council of Ephesus officially condemned the Nestorian heresy, which taught that Jesus is two distinct persons, one divine and one human.

Think about how the church buildings of Ephesus, like its pagan monuments, are gone or in ruins. But the *church* that once flourished in Ephesus was a part of the church triumphant and is still alive. God lives in people, not buildings. We *use* church buildings, and we make them beautiful because God is proclaimed there and He meets His people there. But people come to know God through people. When the church spires, like our high-rise buildings and many-tiered freeways, are all gone, and there is a new heaven and a new earth, those who profess faith in the risen Savior whom Paul proclaimed will still be alive. That should encourage and strengthen us regardless of our circumstances, and keep us faithful in whatever God has called us to do.

What are the Leading Ideas of Ephesians?

Typical of Paul's epistles, this book divides naturally into two halves with a lofty theological section in chapters 1–3 and a practical application section in chapters 4-6. The dominant theme is the relationship between the heavenly Lord Jesus Christ and His earthly body, the church. Christ now reigns *"far above all rule and authority and power and dominion"* (1:21) because *"[God] put all things under His feet"* (1:22). So intimately does Jesus identify with the church that He considers it His body, which He fills with His presence. The enthroned Christ becomes real in the life of believers through faith, and that relationship is established in Christ's love.

Christ's union with the church leads irrevocably to the unity of believers in the church. Those who once were *"far off"* and separated from God *"have been brought near by the blood of Christ"* (2:13). If believers are with Christ, they are also to be like Christ. *"Maintain the unity of the Spirit in the bond of peace"* (4:3) is Paul's imperative to believers. *"He Himself is our peace"* (2:14), for Christ Jesus removes the walls and barriers that formerly divided Jews and Gentiles, and in Himself He draws them together in one Spirit to the Father.

Given the marvelous divine statement of what God has done, Paul directs believers to: *"Walk in a manner worthy of the calling to which you have been called"* (4:1). He provides a series of examples showing how believers can honor Christ rightly, but the goal is never to earn merit through morality. Paul does not just see believers as *nice people*; he envisions them as *new people* who *"all attain to the unity of the faith and of the knowledge of the Son of God, to mature manhood, to the measure of the stature of the fullness of Christ"* (4:13).

Personalize this lesson.

 At the beginning of His earthly ministry Jesus called disciples, saying, *"Follow Me."* After His resurrection He said again to Peter, *"You follow Me!"* (John 21:22). To follow Him is, in Paul's words, to *"walk in a manner worthy of the calling to which you have been called"* (Ephesians 4:1). Christ calls each of us now to follow Him. In what way would you like to follow Jesus more closely?

Hope for the Hopeless
Ephesians 1:1-14

Memorize God's Word: Ephesians 1:3.

❖ Ephesians 1:1-3—Paul Greets the Saints and Praises God

1. Paul introduces himself in 1:1 as *"an apostle of Christ Jesus,"* and on the basis of that fact gives authoritative instructions to the Christians who will read his letter. What convinced Paul that he was an apostle?

   a. Acts 26:12-18 _____

   _____

   b. 1 Corinthians 9:1-2_____

   _____

   c. 2 Corinthians 12:11-12_____

   _____

2. Ephesians is written to *"saints"* (1:1). This word comes from the Greek word for *holy*. According to Romans 1:6-7, how would you define a *saint*?

   _____

3. Read Ephesians 1:3 and list at least three spiritual blessings for which you could praise and thank God.

   _____

   _____

❖ Ephesians 1:4-6—Chosen Before Birth

4. What was God's plan for us when He chose us? (See also Romans 8:29.)

_____

_____

_____

_____

5. What does it mean to *"be holy"* (Ephesians 1:4)? See Colossians 1:22; Titus 2:11-14.

_____

_____

_____

6. Ephesians 1:4-5 tells us that *"in love* [God] *predestined us for adoption"* by faith in Christ. On what basis are we *"adopted"* (1:5)?

_____

_____

_____

7. Read Ephesians 1:6 and 2:8. Define *grace* in your own words.

_____

_____

_____

❖ Ephesians 1:7-10—The Cross, God's Means of Grace

8. What does *redemption* mean? Use a dictionary if you like.

_____

_____

_____

9. Using 1:9-10, record how you would explain God's plan to a friend.

_____

_____

_____

_____

10. Read Colossians 1:15-20, and list some ways that Christ is head of *"all things ... in heaven and ... on earth"* (Ephesians 1:10).

_____

_____

_____

_____

❖ Ephesians 1:11-14—Believers' Inheritance

11. Ephesians 1:11 says we were chosen and predestined according to God's plan. According to John 15:16 and Ephesians 2:10, what is our place in that plan?

_____

_____

12. According to 1:13, how can you be *"sealed with the promised Holy Spirit"*?

_____

_____

13. What assurance has God given us that He will forgive our sins and give us eternal salvation?

_____

_____

_____

_____

Apply what you have learned. As we travel through the joys and challenges of life, we sometimes have to pause and wonder what the deeper significance is to our existence. Jewish playwright Leo Rosten said, "I can't believe that the purpose of life is to be happy. I think the purpose of life is to be useful, to be compassionate. It is above all to matter, to stand for something, to have made some difference that you lived at all."

This first chapter of Ephesians reveals that each of us, if we belong to Christ, is, indeed, part of a grand plan for the universe. We were worked into that plan *"before the foundation of the world"* (1:4). As you continue studying this lesson, let your Creator speak to you about your unique place in His plan.

Lesson 2 Commentary

Hope for the Hopeless
Ephesians 1:1-14

Paul's Beginning Salutation (Ephesians 1:1-3)

Paul identifies himself as *"an apostle of Christ Jesus"* (1:1). *Apostle* derives from the Greek verb that means *to send with a commission or specific purpose*. The apostle states his commission to be by the sovereign *"will of God"* (1:1).

Paul calls his readers *"the saints"* and *"faithful."* The root of the word *saint* is *holy*, that is, something *set apart for special use*. Something is holy because of God's choosing and using, not because of intrinsic or earned merits. *Faithful* means *adhering firmly to a cause, idea, or person*. Faithfulness is personified in Jesus, and He enables believers to be faithful when they trust in Him. Paul concludes the salutation by wishing his readers *"grace … and peace"* (1:2), which come *"from God our Father and the Lord Jesus Christ."*

Paul adds, *"Blessed be the God and Father of our Lord Jesus Christ, who has blessed us in Christ with every spiritual blessing in the heavenly places"* (1:3). Paul is thrilled by what God has revealed and accomplished in Jesus Christ. Nine times, he links his praise and *"blessing"* with *"in Christ."* The spiritual blessings received, the love and forgiveness that come, the choosing, and the hope are not inalienable rights, but gifts of grace and blessings that come only *"in Christ."*

Chosen Before the Foundation of the World (Ephesians 1:4-6)

Paul says that *"before the foundation of the world,"* God *"chose"* and *"predestined"* all who are *"in Christ"* by faith to be beneficiaries of His blessings. God did not begrudgingly allocate Gentiles a place in His family, but *"according to the purpose of His will"* He ordained them to be

His spiritual children! In Christ there is no *"dividing wall"* (2:14) between people. Rather, God *"predestined us"*—Jews and Gentiles—for "sonship."

Predestination is often misunderstood to be the expression of a blind, determining force, or of an arbitrary God who determines eternal fates of individuals, and perhaps even nations, prior to and in spite of their behavior. But the Bible presents a God who acts, not reacts—who creates, calls, and consummates according to His eternal purpose. Before anything was, there was the divine purpose, and all God does in history executes the divine will. Sin and evil may hinder its progress, but *cannot* change it.

In this passage, Paul does not state that some are predestined to damnation. He teaches that God eternally included Gentiles (whom Jews thought to be damned) in His salvation plan. Thus, predestination—at least as seen in Ephesians—must be understood as the *divine positive*; God works for His creation, not against it.

Paul emphasizes that God chose us with an intention and purpose, namely, that we become morally upright—*"holy and blameless"*—that is, that we participate in and demonstrate God's character. That expectation is inseparably linked to His original choosing.

Finally, one cannot speak of predestination without speaking of Jesus, the human face of God, the One through whom God executes His eternal pleasure. In Christ one sees not raw power, but power expressed in love. God chose His own before the foundation of the world. God wills that they share in His joy, love, and life. *God is for us* (Romans 8:31). In predestination, it might be said that He "stacks the deck" in our favor. Predestination, when rightly understood, results in *"the praise of His glorious grace"* (Ephesians 1:6).

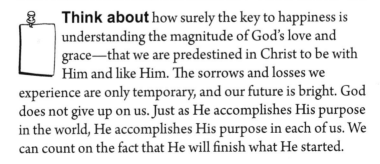

Think about how surely the key to happiness is understanding the magnitude of God's love and grace—that we are predestined in Christ to be with Him and like Him. The sorrows and losses we experience are only temporary, and our future is bright. God does not give up on us. Just as He accomplishes His purpose in the world, He accomplishes His purpose in each of us. We can count on the fact that He will finish what He started.

The Cross, God's Means of Grace (Ephesians 1:7-10)

Christ's death on the Cross makes grace possible. His death provides *"redemption"* and *"forgiveness"* because of *"the riches of* [God's] *grace"* (1:7). The meaning of the phrase *"through His blood"* would be puzzling if not for the precedent of the Passover lamb, whose blood on the doorposts of the Hebrews' homes in Egypt was the sign of their redemption from slavery and death. Verse 7, then, affirms that the Cross was not an afterthought or a deviation in the divine plan, but the very heart of it. Were it not for the Cross, God's grace could not be known in all its richness, nor could redemption and forgiveness be experienced in all their fullness.

"The mystery of [God's] *will"* is a key phrase. Christ's Cross transformed religion from *"mystery"* to knowledge of God's will and the freedom to praise and serve Him. The mystery became known not because of any ability or brilliance on man's part, but because God chose to reveal His will and His essential character. The marvel is that God revealed not something, but *Someone*—Jesus Christ, His Son.

The purpose of this revelation was *"to unite all things in Him, things in heaven and things on earth"* (1:10). The revelation of Jesus Christ was *the* moment, *the* event for which God had been planning, directing, and waiting since the beginning of time. In addition to creating the world, God has a purpose with regard to it, a purpose known only in Jesus Christ.

Believers' Inheritance (Ephesians 1:11-14)

In 1:12, the phrase *"we who were the first to hope in Christ"* refers to the Jews, but it does not imply Jewish superiority. It simply states that the Jews had the Messianic hope first. The Gentiles, however, *"heard the word of truth* [the gospel]*,"* they *"believed,"* and they *"were sealed with the promised Holy Spirit"* (1:13). Hearing, believing, being sealed—these are still the three steps to salvation. Paul says the Holy Spirit *"is the guarantee of our inheritance"* (1:14). Paul is saying that even now the believer has the Holy Spirit as God's "down payment," the promise of *"the redemption of those who are God's possession"* (1:14, NIV).

Personalize this lesson.

☑ Believers are God's possession. He created us; He redeemed us; He sustains us. Ephesians 1:1-14 reveals God's benevolent purpose for creation and states that we have a part in it. When we contemplate the universe, whose spaces unfold before us through modern discoveries, we see something of God's limitless power. When we consider the complexities of our bodies, we see something of God's care for the minute details of our existence. Considering all this, aren't we foolish when we allow anxiety to dominate our thinking? We belong to God, and He takes care of His own. Praise Him for what He has already done for us in Jesus. Thank Him and praise Him for the riches of His grace!

Lesson 3

Knowing the God Who First Knew Us
Ephesians 1:15-23

❖ **Ephesians 1:15-16—Paul Prays for the Ephesians**

1. What two characteristics of the Ephesian Christians prompted Paul's prayer of thanksgiving?

   _____

   _____

2. In your own words, what did Paul ask God to do for the Ephesian Christians (1:17-19)?

   _____

   _____

3. In the chart below list the types of things you most often pray that God will do for other Christians. Put an "S" by the items that relate to their spiritual health and a "P" by the things that relate to their physical or material well-being.

Things I pray for most often:	S/P

❖ Ephesians 1:17—To Know God

4. How is the Trinity revealed in this verse?

   _____

   _____

5. What does this verse say that the Holy Spirit gives us?

   _____

   _____

   _____

6. Read John 16:13-16. What did Jesus tell His disciples about the Holy Spirit?

   _____

   _____

7. What does it mean to have *"revelation in the knowledge of Him"*?

   a. John 14:8-11 _____

   _____

   b. Philippians 3:10 _____

   _____

   c. 1 John 2:4-6 _____

   _____

❖ Ephesians 1:18—To Know Hope

8. The word *hope* is often used for something we desire but have some doubt about receiving or achieving. However, the Bible uses *hope* as a *confident future reality*. What do the following verses tell us about the hope God offers believers?

   a. Acts 24:15 _____

   _____

   b. 1 John 3:1-3 _____

   _____

9. What do these verses tell us about our *"inheritance"* as
    Christians?

    a. Romans 8:17 _____

    _____

    b. James 2:5 _____

    _____

❖ Ephesians 1:19-23—To Experience Power

10. What four things can you find in 1:19-23 that God
    accomplished through the *"immeasurable greatness of His power"*?

    a. _____
    b. _____
    c. _____
    d. _____

11. What sort of things in life do we need this power for, according
    to these verses?

    a. Romans 8:12-14 _____

    _____

    _____

    b. Philippians 1:29 _____

    _____

    c. James 4:7 _____

    _____

12. The power that God makes available to believers is the same
    power that was able to raise Jesus from the dead. What problems
    and challenges do you face today that could use such power?

    _____

    _____

    _____

13. What difference does it make for you today that Jesus has been seated at God's right hand? (See Romans 8:34-39.)

_____

_____

❖ Ephesians 1:21-23—God Exalted Christ

14. What do the following verses tell you about the authority of Christ Jesus?

a. Matthew 28:18 _____

_____

b. 1 Corinthians 15:24-28 _____

_____

15. What does it mean for Christ to be *"head"* of the church (Ephesians 1:22-23)? (See also Colossians 1:18.)

_____

_____

Apply what you have learned. As we mature spiritually, our relationship with God the Father changes. We appreciate His wisdom and His ways more—as those who have loving earthly parents often do. As we study and obey His Word and respond to Him in prayer, our faith will grow. And so will our intimacy with Him! He deeply desires this. If you do too, keep asking Him to *"give you the Spirit of wisdom and of revelation in the knowledge of Him"* (Ephesians 1:17).

Knowing the God Who First Knew Us
Ephesians 1:15-23

Paul's Prayer (Ephesians 1:15-19)

In the second part of chapter 1, Paul moves from giving glory to God to praying for the Ephesians. He prays because he has heard of their *"faith in the Lord Jesus"* and their *"love toward all the saints"* (1:15). It was characteristic of the apostle, a pastor whose heart was zealous for his congregations, to thank God for what they already were before charging them with what they ought to become.

Paul addresses God as *"the God of our Lord Jesus Christ,"* who is also *"the Father of glory"* (1:17). Paul prays that *"[God] may give you the Spirit of wisdom and revelation in the knowledge of Him"*—that they would receive spiritual insight. We do not acquire knowledge of God by human effort; it is a gift of God. Having the right attitude and a teachable spirit help make God's job of revealing truth easier, but ultimately it depends on the Holy Spirit, who alone bestows *"wisdom and revelation"* (1:17). The Spirit reveals Christ. He (literally in Greek) *lifts the veil.*

Paul prays for the Spirit to make that inner transformation in a person's life that allows one to *know* God more intimately. Paul's word for *"knowledge"* cannot be interpreted to mean that the Spirit will make Christians smarter, but that the Spirit will give inner enlightenment, that *"the eyes of your hearts* [be] *enlightened"* (1:18). Divine illumination is deeper than an intellectual process. It illumines a person's heart and will.

The enlightenment Paul desires for them is threefold: *"the hope to which He has called you … the riches of His glorious inheritance"* (1:18), and *"the immeasurable greatness of His power"* (1:19). For Paul, hope's substance depends entirely on its object. In Colossians 1:27, Paul says that *"Christ in you* [is] *the hope of glory."* And, regarding *"the riches of His glorious inheritance in the saints"* (Ephesians 1:18), the reference is not exclusively to our future but to something on a grander scale—Christ's cosmic lordship, of which our inheritance is only a small part. Paul has in mind the power that God used in raising Jesus from the dead and seating Him at His right hand (1:20), the same power that makes Him the supreme head of the universe. Interestingly, this threefold knowledge embraces all eternity. *"The hope to which He has called you"* directs us to the past. *"The riches of His glorious inheritance"* directs us to the future. And *"the immeasurable greatness of His power"* directs us to the present.

Christ, Lord of the Universe, Lord of the Church (Ephesians 1:20-23)

God has seated Christ *"in the heavenly places"* (1:20). In 6:12, Paul states that believers are presently engaged in a battle with the powers of evil *"in the heavenly places."* *"Heavenly places"* here obviously varies from the concept of heaven as a place of everlasting joy in God's presence. The five occurrences of the phrase in Ephesians appear to define it as a region above the physical, empirical world in which we live, a supra-terrestrial realm in which Christ reigns and from which He is overcoming all powers that oppose His fullness and final purpose.

In verse 21, Paul identifies the powers that are subordinated to Christ as *"all rule and authority and power and dominion, and above every name that is named."* At Creation, God decreed of man, *"let them have dominion ... over all the earth"* (Genesis 1:26). The rulership or dominion that God appointed for man as His steward over creation, but that man forfeited by sin, is now given to Christ. Christ's dominion is not only over the earth, however, but over all the powers in the heavenly realms. Thus, Christ has fulfilled in His person the destiny for which human beings were created!

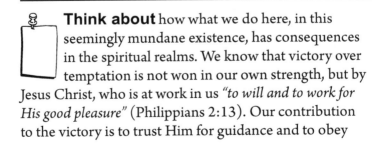

Think about how what we do here, in this seemingly mundane existence, has consequences in the spiritual realms. We know that victory over temptation is not won in our own strength, but by Jesus Christ, who is at work in us *"to will and to work for His good pleasure"* (Philippians 2:13). Our contribution to the victory is to trust Him for guidance and to obey

Him when it comes. The victories won by mighty armies
are of less significance in the heavenly realms than the
unnoticed victories over temptation and sin won by
anonymous believers.

Paul's crowning thought in Ephesians 1 is: *"God ... gave* [Christ] *as
head over all things to the church, which is His body, the fullness of Him
who fills all in all"* (1:22-23). God has elevated and enthroned Christ
not only because of the honor of which He is supremely worthy, but
also in order to establish Him as head of the church. The Greek word
for *head* encompasses the meaning of *source* as well as *chief.* In 1:10,
God's purpose—*"to unite all things in Him, things in heaven and things
on earth"*—is first mentioned. Now the means by which God will
accomplish this comprehensive program is disclosed; the agent for
change is Christ's body, the church.

Christ is the head of the church, and as His body He fills it with His
"spiritual lifeblood." The church, in turn, participates in the life of her
ascended Lord. As Christ has filled the church with Himself, so the
church is to allow the riches of Christ's presence to overflow into the
world. The church, then, is the vessel by which Christ accomplishes His
saving activity in the world and *"fills everything in every way"* (1:23, NIV).
God and His Messiah, Jesus, are present in the church and fill it, for the
benefit of all creation. Paul is not saying here that the church has a role of
world domination, but rather that the church is filled by and is a servant
of her Lord, Christ Jesus. God calls His people to demonstrate His
presence, love, and power for the redemption of the world.

Personalize this lesson.

☑ The New Testament ties the manifestation of God's glory to the Cross, and the right to rule to the willingness to serve. In His high priestly prayer, the night before His crucifixion, Jesus began, *"Father, the time has come. Glorify Your Son, that Your Son may glorify You"* (John 17:1). The time that had come was the time of His death. In utter opposition to everything the world regards as glory, God was glorified by the sacrificial death of His Son. It was the culmination of Jesus' life, a life spent serving others—healing, teaching, touching, being available to all who sought Him.

When Jesus comes again, it will be in a different kind of glory—in all His authority and the splendor of heaven. God assures us that we will share that glory. In the meantime, we share the glory of Jesus' earthly life, which means that we rule as we serve and often have our greatest opportunity to glorify God as we suffer. What opportunities has God given you to serve others and perhaps even sacrifice for them? As you follow Jesus' lead in ministering to others this way, you show that you are truly a member of His church, *"which is His body, the fullness of Him who fills all in all"* (Ephesians 1:23).

Lesson 4

The Key to Salvation
Ephesians 2:1-10

Memorize God's Word: Ephesians 2:8-9.

❖ Ephesians 2:1-2—Paul Reminds the Ephesians of Their Former Condition

1. How do the following passages reveal that we are *"dead"* in our sins?

    a. Genesis 2:15-17; 3:6-11, 19 _____

    _____

    b. Romans 3:23-24; 6:23_____

    _____

2. Note the description of the culture that these Ephesians grew up in (2:2). Comment on what each phrase adds to your understanding of their former condition.

    a. *"in which you once walked"*_____

    _____

    _____

    b. *"following the course of this world"*_____

    _____

    _____

    c. *"following the prince of the power of the air"* _____

    _____

    _____

❖ Ephesians 2:3—Paul Comments on the Former Condition of the Ephesians

3. What is God's evaluation of the human condition?

    a. Ephesians 2:3 _____

    _____

    b. Jeremiah 17:9 _____

    _____

    c. Romans 3:9-18 _____

    _____

4. What is God's attitude toward sin?

    a. Romans 1:18 _____

    _____

    b. 1 Corinthians 6:9-10 _____

    _____

❖ Ephesians 2:4-6—Paul Gives the Ephesians Some Encouraging News

5. Remembering our condition (revealed in 2:3), state what you see as the significance of the fact that 2:4 begins with the words "But God." (See also Romans 5:8.)

    _____

    _____

6. What motivates God to extend mercy to sinners?

    _____

    _____

7. God is *"rich in mercy"* (Ephesians 2:4). Write your own definition of *mercy*, using a dictionary if you choose.

    _____

    _____

8. How can we experience God's mercy when we have sinned?

    a. Psalm 32:1-5 _____

    _____

    b. 1 John 1:9 _____

    _____

❖ Ephesians 2:7—Paul States God's Reason for Acting

9. What purpose does God have in mind for your future?

    _____

    _____

10. How is the phrase *"immeasurable riches of His grace"* significant to you? (See also 1 Peter 1:3-4.)

    _____

    _____

11. Write a definition of *grace*, using a dictionary if you choose.

    _____

    _____

❖ Ephesians 2:8-10—Paul Explains God's Reason for Acting As He Did

12. Because we are saved *"by grace ... through faith,"* what is our part in salvation?

    _____

    _____

13. Paul explicitly states why God chose to save us *"by grace ... through faith."* What is the stated reason (2:9)?

    _____

    _____

14. What do you learn about God's attitude toward pride and boasting from Proverbs 16:18-19?

_____

_____

15. a. Because we do not earn salvation by good works, what is the place of good works in God's plan for a believer in:

    1) Ephesians 2:10? _____

    _____

    _____

    2) 1 Peter 2:12? _____

    _____

    _____

  b. How do you think an understanding of these Scriptures should impact your daily life?

_____

_____

_____

_____

Apply what you have learned. God has carefully planned and executed our salvation in a way that will not encourage us to stumble and fall. Remember that a haughty spirit goes before a fall (Proverbs 16:18) and that God puts a haughty look at the very top of the list of things He hates (Proverbs 6:16-19). Do you hunger and thirst after God enough to swallow your pride and come to Him for the salvation that He alone can give? Do you want to experience new life enough to admit that your old life is far from perfect? Just as pride goes before a fall, so humility goes before a glorious new life in Christ.

Lesson 4 Commentary

The Key to Salvation
Ephesians 2:1-10

Strength to Face the Past (Ephesians 2:1-3)

More than any other passage in the Bible, Ephesians 2:1-10 articulates Christianity's most famous and important doctrine—salvation by grace through faith. Paul refers to spiritual death because of the *"sins in which you once walked"* (2:2). He is referring here not just to individual preferences for a lifestyle of faithlessness or disobedience; he is referring to a life that conforms with powerful world forces almost beyond the sinner's comprehension. Through the Fall, the world became subject to wicked spirit powers that control this evil, transitory age. This subjection lies behind the terminology of 2:2, *"the course of this world"* and *"the prince of the power of the air."* The battle takes place not merely on a physical plane; it involves spiritual superpowers.

Everyone is guilty of unbelief and disobedience; all incur divine wrath because of it. We *"were by nature children of wrath, like the rest of mankind"* (2:3). Paul does not say that the Gentiles were inherently sinners, while the Jews were actually good people who merely made mistakes from time to time. Instead, Paul uses an all-inclusive *"we all."* The Jews, the most religious and moral people the world had then known, and the Ephesian Gentiles were equally *"by nature children of wrath."* *"By nature"* refers to the essence of a thing.

Paul adds another phrase—*"of our flesh"* (2:3). The Greek word for *flesh* is *sarx*, which does not mean physical or sensual nature, but *human nature*. Apart from Jesus' grace, the sentence of divine judgment hangs over every individual.

Think about how even the nicest, most respectable, most cultured people—apart from Jesus Christ—are no better in God's eyes than those whose sins are visible, contemptible, and punishable by law. It is easy to spot obvious sins in others, and it is equally easy to overlook our own. The truth is that by nature we are all sinners. Try as we might, our best efforts are warped by pride, selfishness, and lack of love. The beginning of spiritual maturity comes when we admit our inability to be perfect, when we personalize the good news of the gospel, when each of us realizes that Christ died for *my* selfishness, *my* bad temper, *my* lies, *my* meanness, or *my* insensitivity to the needs and pain of others—and when we finally see that without Him *my* case is hopeless.

The Triumph of Grace (Ephesians 2:4-7)

Paul switches the focus from our human inadequacy to divine remedy. *"But God"*—those two words are indispensable. No matter how ugly, tragic, or deeply rooted human sin may be, Christians do not need to allow it the final word. The one word in which grace and mercy find their most perfect expression is *agape*. Agape is that unique kind of love that is prompted neither by merit on the part of its object nor by need on its giver's behalf. Agape expresses God's character. It is unconditional, unwarranted, and unexpected love. Paul refers to our former *"dead*[ness]*"* not because he wants to dwell on that depressing fact, but in order to accentuate God's grace, which *"made us alive together with Christ"* (2:5).

Grace goes beyond inner enlightenment or liberation. In grace, God includes believers in His blessings to Christ, whom God *"raised ... from the dead and seated ... at His right hand in the heavenly places"* (1:20). We will experience this fully in the future, but even now we can know it in part. Salvation is now a reality; but in 2:7, Paul uses the future tense: *"so that in the coming ages* [God] *might show the immeasurable riches of His grace."* Salvation must always be received in the present, in the universal church, the community of believers through whom God witnesses to each age of *"the immeasurable riches of His grace in kindness toward us in Christ Jesus"* (2:7). God calls people to salvation wherever believers stand up as faithful witnesses to Christ, wherever His Word is proclaimed. He calls them on the basis of something that happened in the past, but it also points to a glorious future.

Salvation for Works, Not by Works (Ephesians 2:8-10)

Paul repeats and expands the idea that he briefly introduced in verse 5: *"by grace you have been saved."* Especially important is the verb tense: *"you have been saved."* Paul does not say, "You shall be saved," as though salvation were a process yet to be accomplished; nor "you were saved," as though salvation were fully completed. The verb tense carries the distinct meaning that something began in the past, continues in the present, and will continue into the future.

The most important thing to be said of salvation, of course, is that *"this is not your own doing; it is the gift of God"* (2:8). It is true that faith is the human response to grace, but faith can no more take credit for salvation than a prisoner can take credit for freedom because he walked from his cell once the door had been unlocked. Paul underscores this in verse 9: *"not a result of works, so that no one may boast."* It is dangerous for humans to think that God somehow owes us salvation. No matter how subtle, this attitude of self-righteousness shuts the door on grace. Paul establishes our "deadness" in Ephesians 2:1-3 and 5. Something dead cannot act in its own behalf. Each of us must first acknowledge our "deadness" if we are to receive grace, which is quite literally resurrection from the dead. God intends that we become like Him, but we can achieve this only through His gift. We are, and always shall be, God's *"workmanship"* (2:10).

Paul closes by putting works in their proper context: *"We are ... created in Christ Jesus for good works"* (2:10). If we are most emphatically not saved *by* works, we are just as emphatically saved *for* them! We are saved by grace alone, but the grace that saves does not remain alone. It bears *"fruit."* These are works, or *"fruit,"* which *"God prepared beforehand, that we should walk in them."*

Personalize this lesson.

☑ Although Paul reaches sublime heights in his exposition of all God has done for us in Christ, he doesn't leave us there. We will not be healthy Christians if we remain too long in a rarified atmosphere of spiritual loftiness. We need to come down from the mountaintop, and the world needs us to come down. Our world needs us to bring God's insight, strength, and comfort. The works that God has prepared for us to do include, perhaps above all else, our relationships with the people around us. Many of them are concealing deep wounds and need an understanding listener. Some are Christians who are having a hard time trusting God. Many do not know Christ. God loves them, but they are lost without Him. What can we do? We can live our lives *"to the praise of His glorious grace, with which He has blessed us in the Beloved"* (1:6), and we can do the *"good works which God prepared beforehand, that we should walk in them"* (2:10). Talk about joy! Talk about fulfillment!

Christ the Bridge Builder
Ephesians 2:11-22

❖ **Ephesians 2:11-13—God's Welcome to Outsiders**

1. Read Genesis 17:9-14. What did circumcision mean to the Jewish people?

   _____

   _____

2. Use a dictionary to define *covenant*.

   _____

   _____

   _____

3. From Romans 9:3-5, give your understanding of the advantages of being a descendant of Abraham.

   _____

   _____

   _____

   _____

4. Read Genesis 12:1-3; and Galatians 3:29. What relevance does the truth found in these verses have for today's Gentiles?

   _____

   _____

   _____

   _____

5. According to Ephesians 2:13 and John 12:32, what brings us
    "near" to God?

    _____

    _____

6. What does it mean to you to be near to God?

    _____

    _____

    _____

❖ Ephesians 2:14-16—Jesus Makes Peace

7. Jesus is called *"our peace"* in verse 14. Peace has many
    expressions. What did the prophets say about Him bringing
    peace?

    a. Isaiah 9:6-7_____

        _____

    b. Micah 5:4-5 _____

        _____

8. What did the angels say? (See Luke 2:13-14.)

    _____

    _____

    _____

9. What did Paul say? (See Romans 5:1.)

    _____

    _____

    _____

10. What did Jesus say? (See John 14:27.)

    _____

    _____

    _____

11. From Ephesians 2:14-16, record the things that Jesus has accomplished for you personally if you are *"in Him."*

_____

_____

_____

_____

❖ Ephesians 2:17-20—All Have Access to the Father

12. Continue your list begun in response to Question 11, using verses 17-20.

_____

_____

_____

_____

13. In this present age, how are Jews as well as Gentiles saved (brought into *"the household of God,"* 2:19)? (See also Romans 10:9-10; Ephesians 2:8.)

_____

_____

_____

_____

14. a. What is the *"foundation of the apostles and prophets"*? (See 2 Peter 1:19-21.) _____

_____

_____

   b. How can that foundation strengthen us? _____

_____

_____

❖ Ephesians 2:20-22—God's Holy Temple

15. The cornerstone gives a building its strength and stability. From

the following verses, what are some benefits of having Christ as our chief cornerstone?

   a.   1 Corinthians 3:9-15 (Note: Here, Christ is called *the foundation* rather than *the cornerstone.*)

   _____

   _____

   b.   Ephesians 2:21-22 _____

   _____

   _____

   c.   1 Peter 2:4-6 _____

   _____

   _____

16. God has made us into His *"holy temple."* What are some practical implications that this has for our conduct?

   a.   1 Corinthians 6:18-20 _____

   _____

   _____

   b.   2 Corinthians 6:14–7:1 _____

   _____

   _____

Apply what you have learned. Does your "temple" need a spring cleaning, or is it holy and pure? Are you at peace with other people, or do you have a lot of accumulated "stuff" cluttering your relationships that you could sort through and dispose of? Do you have attitude or behavior patterns that need to be cleansed by *"confess*[ing *your*] *sins"* (1 John 1:9) and *"washing of water with the word"* (Ephesians 5:26)? Make a list of the things you would like to have God's help in cleaning out and begin to pray for the courage and wisdom to follow His leading.

Christ the Bridge Builder
Ephesians 2:11-22

Christ the Bridge Builder (Ephesians 2:11-13)

Paul understood that God desires absolute equality within the church. Thus, his letter to the Ephesians calls believers to commit their lives to the continuing work of reconciliation. Within the church, Christians have the privilege and responsibility of demonstrating to the world what Christian unity means.

Paul refers to Gentiles as those who are *"called 'the uncircumcision,'"* demonstrating that the Jewish claim to superiority is only skin deep. In 2:12, Paul reminds the Gentiles that they were once *"alienated from the commonwealth of Israel and strangers to the covenants of the promise."* Socially and theologically, they were separated from God's covenant. As a consequence, they had *"no hope and* [were] *without God in the world."*

The hallmark of Israel's faith was that it looked forward to Messiah's arrival and provision of salvation. But the Gentiles were relegated to life *"in the world,"* without God, hence without hope. *"Without God"* means *without the one, true God.* In this context, *"world"* means *unredeemed humanity.* With this negative assessment, Paul characterizes the Gentiles' past. But in Christ, all this has changed. Paul says, *"But now,"* and proceeds with a statement of contrast: *once* you were *far; now* you are *near.* The radical change from exclusion to inclusion is due to no virtue on the Gentiles' part; the change is accomplished through *"the blood of Christ"* (2:13).

Leviticus 17:11 states that *"the life of the flesh is in the blood."* When Paul speaks of Christ's blood, therefore, he means that Christ gave His life to restore Gentiles to fellowship with Him. Giving His lifeblood activates grace, enabling God to be merciful and just in offering relationship to Jews and Gentiles.

Think about how, by shedding His blood, Christ not only gave us a transfusion, He gave us His life. When we were *"dead in ... trespasses and sins"* (Ephesians 2:1), we were as lifeless, spiritually, as a body without blood is lifeless physically. His shed blood can remove our deadly "sin-sickness" just as a total transfusion can remove a deadly incompatible blood type. The spiritual life we now live, therefore, is His life, just as surely as if His blood flowed through our veins. We still think, reason, feel, decide; we retain our individuality. We are not less than we were, but more, because we are filled with His life. *"I have been crucified with Christ. It is no longer I who live, but Christ who lives in me. And the life I now live in the flesh I live by faith in the Son of God, who loved me and gave Himself for me"* (Galatians 2:20).

Breaking Down the Wall of Division (Ephesians 2:14-18)

"He Himself is our peace, who has made us both one and has broken down in His flesh the dividing wall of hostility" (2:14). Peace is a person—Jesus Christ. The word *peace*, derived from the Hebrew *shalom*, does not mean simply an absence of hostility or "peaceful coexistence." It refers to possessing and experiencing well-being with God and others even in the midst of the worst circumstances.

Christ *"has made us both one."* The key image is *"the dividing wall."* Christ demolished that barrier and the *"hostility"* with it. The temple's dividing wall expressed the separation that Christ radically eliminated. In Christ, all barriers between peoples have been *"broken down in His flesh."* This phrase refers to Christ's death on the cross, by which God created one new community.

Paul identifies the wall as *"the law of commandments expressed in ordinances"* (2:15). Christ *"broke down"* that wall—not in a fit of anger or righteous indignation, but in order to create. In the Bible, creation is an act of God. In this instance, His purpose was to *"create in Himself one new man in place of two, so making peace."* The word *"two"* refers to Jews and Gentiles, and the Greek explicitly states that *Christ* creates *"one new man."* It is not for believers to make peace—we may receive God's peace, and we are summoned to keep peace—but Christ is always the author of peace.

The peace by which Gentiles and Jews are reconciled is a direct consequence of peace with God through the Cross of Calvary. The Cross—which reconciles us with God—also reconciles us with others, and this truth makes walls of division impossible for Christians. The Cross of Christ *"kill[ed] the hostility."* No believer stands outside or alone, but *"in Christ"* belongs to God. Those who are *"in one body"* (2:16) and those who *"have access in one Spirit to the Father"* (2:18) are those who are in the church, the body of believers.

God's House Is Built From the Rubble of the Dividing Wall (Ephesians 2:19-22)

Paul concludes chapter 2 by defining a new structure made up of reconciled humanity. *"So then,"* says Paul, *"you are no longer strangers and aliens, but you are fellow citizens with the saints and members of the household of God"* (2:19). For Gentiles, this is the exact opposite of their former condition, *"alienated from the commonwealth of Israel and strangers"* (2:12)! God has brought His family together. Warmth, care, and belonging have replaced strife and hostility.

Christian fellowship is *"built"* on the preaching of the *"apostles and prophets"* (2:20). The *building* metaphor reveals that the family members are not inhabitants of God's house; they *are* God's house. They are the building blocks for God's dwelling. Jesus is the building's chief stone, the precious tested stone in Zion, which the Old Testament prophets foretold the Messiah would be.

Ephesians 2:21-22 reveal that the church will not be completed until Christ's return. The emphasis lies on what the church is becoming—*"a holy temple ... a dwelling place for God."* The growth or process is not automatic, however. Chapter 2 concludes with a metaphor that carries the Ephesians' thinking into the future, revealing something they have not seen or been before. Christians must not look solely to the past to learn who they are. They must also follow God into the future, for God is making all things new.

Personalize this lesson.

☑ The underlying theme in this entire passage is reconciliation. Christians are people who are reconciled—first to God, then within ourselves, and then to others. Once we respond to God's love, we should begin to respond to each other in love—*"Beloved, if God so loved us, we also ought to love one another"* (1 John 4:11). Differences with others, times when we feel hurt or angry or critical, are opportunities to obey what God says rather than our feelings. Broken relationships grieve God. They weaken His temple in the same way cracks in a building weaken the entire structure. There is nothing wrong with our foundation or cornerstone. How, specifically, could you contribute positively toward making the building a stable, holy temple?

Lesson 6

Paul and His Ministry
Ephesians 3:1-13

❖ **Ephesians 3:1-2—Paul Is a "Gifted" Prisoner**

1. Record what these passages tell about Paul being a prisoner.

   a. Acts 21:27-36 _____

   _____

   _____

   b. Ephesians 6:19-20 _____

   _____

   _____

   c. 2 Timothy 1:8-12 _____

   _____

   _____

2. What does Galatians 2:1-9 tell you about why Paul focuses so intently upon bringing the gospel to the Gentiles?

   _____

   _____

   _____

❖ **Ephesians 3:3-6—Paul Writes a Mystery Story**

3. What is the *"mystery"* that Paul refers to, according to 3:6?

   _____

   _____

4. Re-read Ephesians 2:11-18 to help you understand the broad significance of the three terms Paul uses in 3:6 to describe Gentile believers. What does it mean to you that you are:

   a. *"fellow heirs* [with Israel]*"*? (See also Titus 3:7.) _____

   _____

   _____

   b. *"members of the same body"*? _____

   _____

   _____

   c. *"partakers of the promise in Christ Jesus"*? (See 2:18; 2 Peter 1:4.) _____

   _____

   _____

❖ Ephesians 3:7-9—Paul Explains His Mission

5. Paul says, *"Of this gospel I was made a minister."* How does he say he is able to accomplish this task?

   _____

6. Based on the following passages, why did Paul consider himself to be *"the very least of all the saints"*? Was this just an example of exaggerated humility?

   a. Galatians 1:13-17 _____

   _____

   _____

   b. 1 Timothy 1:12-15 _____

   _____

   _____

7. How are you encouraged by God's use of Paul?

   _____

   _____

❖ Ephesians 3:10-12—God Reveals His Intentions

8. What do we learn of God's eternal purposes for us in 1:4, 11?

   _____

   _____

9. How is it possible to approach God with *"boldness and ... confidence"* (3:12) if you know you are less than perfectly holy?

   a. 1 Timothy 2:5 _____

   _____

   b. Hebrews 10:19-23_____

   _____

10. What is the significance for you personally of being able to approach God with boldness and confidence?

   _____

   _____

   _____

   _____

❖ Ephesians 3:13—Paul Speaks of the Glory of Suffering

11. According to the following passages, how could Paul consider suffering to be *glory*?

   a. Philippians 3:10-11_____

   _____

   b. James 1:12 _____

   _____

12. According to the following passages, why does God allow hardship to come into Christians' lives?

   a. Romans 5:3-5 _____

   _____

b. 2 Corinthians 1:3-5_____

_____

c. 1 Peter 1:6-7 _____

_____

Apply what you have learned. While Paul was in prison at various times, he wrote eight books of the New Testament. He repeatedly assured his readers that suffering, when it comes, can accomplish God's purposes in a believer's life. The entire Bible is strangely silent on how to escape suffering, but very articulate about its benefits. Are there principles you can draw from Paul's attitude and accomplishments while suffering that can help you develop what certainly appears to be God's mindset on this "problem of suffering"?

Lesson 6 Commentary

Paul and His Ministry
Ephesians 3:1-13

The Mystery of God's Love for the Gentiles (Ephesians 3:1-6)

Three themes occupy Paul in this passage: *revelation, apostleship,* and *the servant nature of the church.* In 3:2, Paul refers to *"the stewardship of God's grace that was given to me for you."* Here, *grace* refers to God-given *stewardship* or *responsibility.* The explosive truth that God loves the forsaken Gentiles and wills their inclusion in salvation was not something Paul arrived at on his own. It was a *"mystery ... made known to* [him] *by revelation"* (3:3). *Revelation* means *the unveiling or revealing of a truth that cannot otherwise be known.* By *"mystery,"* Paul means God's eternal plan that now must be made known to the Gentiles.

Again, in verse 4, Paul mentions *"the mystery,"* though with two additions. First, it is *"my insight into the mystery,"* thus underscoring Paul's authority. Second, it is *"the mystery of Christ."* God reveals Himself in a Person, Jesus Christ. Jesus both expresses and embodies God's deepest nature, and Gentiles are *"partakers of the promise"* in Him (3:6). Gentiles' full participation in God's plan is startling "new" truth.

This mystery *"was not made known to the sons of men in other generations"* (3:5). Before Christ, God gave only hints about His plan for the Gentiles. Only in Jesus did God choose to reveal His character, His love for the world, and His plan for the salvation of all who would believe. Only *"now,"* through the apostles and prophets, can the mystery be made fully known.

In 3:6, Paul identifies the content of *"this mystery."* *"Gentiles are fellow heirs, members of the same body, and partakers of the promise in Christ Jesus through the gospel."* Gentiles, previously considered strangers to the covenant, are *in Christ*, on equal footing with the Jews. This truth blew the trumpet for a revolution of the first magnitude in the ancient world. Because of sin, all men—Jew and Gentile—stand in *equal need* of salvation, and because of Christ have *equal access* to it!

Think about how the shattered wall of distinction between Jew and Gentile in the body of Christ has wide implications: *"There is neither Jew nor Greek, there is neither slave nor free, there is no male and female, for you are all one in Christ Jesus"* (Galatians 3:28). The church has always struggled—without total success—to obey this truth. Where it has triumphed, there the witness for Christ has been vibrant. Every one of us is involved in a personal struggle to say "No!" to any tendency to categorize, classify, and pigeonhole people. We must never relax—the tendency dies hard!

Paul Explains His Mission (Ephesians 3:7-13)

To the Great Commission of proclaiming salvation to the Gentiles, Paul says emphatically, *"I was made a minister"* (3:7). He focuses on responsibility—to be a servant. Paul knew the example of his Master, for Jesus said, *"the Son of Man came not to be served but to serve, and to give His life"* (Mark 10:45). For Paul, service was a *"gift of God's grace,"* the result of the *"working of His power"* (Ephesians 3:7).

God gave His grace to *"the very least of all the saints"* (3:8). Paul, who considered himself the least worthy, became the one most honored to proclaim grace to the Gentiles. He who was bent on destroying God's church found himself engulfed by God's grace and commissioned to build the church he once tried to destroy.

God gave him grace *"to preach to the Gentiles"* and *"to bring to light* [the mystery] *for everyone."* (3:8-9). God gives grace, in other words, to reveal Himself. What was unknown in ages past, and even now seems like madness—that the Son of God would suffer a shameful death on the Cross in order to save sinners *"far away"* (2:13)—Paul regards as *"the manifold wisdom of God"* (3:10). This has little to do with what the world calls wisdom. In fact, the Cross is the single moment in time when we see with total clarity *"the power ... and the wisdom of God"* (1 Corinthians 1:24).

This wisdom is communicated *"through the church"* (Ephesians 3:10), the human institution given the task of reaching out to a desperately needy world with the message of eternal life. The church's message is directed not only to individuals and social structures, as though the church were dedicated solely to human welfare, but also *"to the rulers and authorities in the heavenly places"* (3:10). The Bible teaches that creation includes angels and demons, spiritual powers beyond our understanding. Ultimately, the church is involved in spiritual combat (6:10).

Paul anchors *"the eternal purpose"* (3:11) of *"the manifold wisdom of God"* (3:10) concretely in Jesus Christ. This means that God's wisdom is not abstract and nebulous. God's wisdom is a Person whose life in the first third of the 1st century AD revealed who God is and how He conducts Himself in the world. God's wisdom is not mere thoughts in His head but works of His hands. Paul expands this idea in 3:12: *"In* [Him] *we have boldness and access with confidence through our faith in Him."* The God revealed in Jesus Christ is One we may approach in *"boldness and ... confidence."*

Paul concludes with an appeal to the Ephesians not to be discouraged by his sufferings, *"which is your glory"* (3:13). The enemy of faith is not suffering or hardship. These, in fact, are the crown and glory of discipleship, for they mean that one is counted worthy to suffer on Christ's behalf. The enemy of faith is *discouragement,* or as the Greek implies, *losing heart.* Paul reminds his readers to look beyond the immediate circumstances. The results of his ministry— his readers' transformed lives—allowed Paul to see his "cost" as their "profit," his *"suffering"* as their *"glory."*

Personalize this lesson.

✓ God's eternal purpose which He accomplished in Jesus Christ is our salvation, we know, but it does not stop there. It even includes making the manifold wisdom of God plain *"to the rulers and authorities in the heavenly places"* (3:10)—a mind-teasing statement that whets the appetite for more information. We are not told anything more about that, but we do know that God is actively involved in achieving His purpose. He acted in the Old Testament. He acted in Jesus. He still acts. He has never abandoned the world He created or the people He called. He intervenes in history. God continues to accomplish His purpose through the lives of believers. On the night before Jesus was crucified, He prayed for His followers: *"As You sent me into the world, so I have sent them into the world"* (John 17:18). We are stewards of God's grace. God is acting through us to accomplish His eternal purpose. What does He want you to do? Ask Him!

Lesson 7

The Power and the Glory
Ephesians 3:14-21

Memorize God's Word: Ephesians 3:20-21.

❖ Ephesians 3:14-17a—Paul Prays for the Ephesians

1. From verses 16 and 17a, what does Paul ask God to do for the Ephesians?

   _____

   _____

2. According to the following verses, what are some of the ways the Holy Spirit strengthens us? Which of these are especially meaningful to you?

   a. John 16:13 _____

   _____

   b. Acts 1:8 _____

   _____

   c. Romans 8:26-27_____

   _____

   d. Romans 15:13_____

   _____

   e. Galatians 5:22-23 _____

   _____

   f. Ephesians 1:17 _____

   _____

3. How would you explain the idea of Christ dwelling in a person's heart by faith?

_____

_____

❖ Ephesians 3:17b-18—To Be Rooted and Grounded in Love

4. a. In his prayer for the Ephesians, Paul uses the imagery of roots. In nature, how does having a strong root system benefit a plant? _____

_____

_____

   b. If a person is the "plant" and God's love is the soil in which he or she is rooted, what would you expect that person's life to be like? _____

_____

_____

5. What four dimensions does Paul use to describe God's love? What do you think he is implying about the magnitude of God's love by using these terms?

_____

_____

6. Why do you think it was so important to Paul that the believers at Ephesus comprehend God's love for them?

_____

_____

_____

7. What difference would being rooted and grounded in God's love and comprehending its magnitude make in your life?

_____

_____

❖ Ephesians 3:19–To Know Christ's Love

8. What is the difference between "knowing about" God
    (Romans 1:20-21) and "knowing" Him (John 10:14-15)?

    _____

    _____

    _____

    _____

9. According to the following passages, how is *"the fullness of God"*
    manifested in believers' lives?

    a. Colossians 2:9-10 _____

    _____

    _____

    b. Colossians 3:12-17 _____

    _____

    _____

❖ Ephesians 3:20-21—Paul's Doxology

10. What is God able to do, according to verse 20? How does this
    knowledge about Him encourage you?

    _____

    _____

    _____

    _____

11. What does each of the following passages teach about God's
    willingness and power to answer prayer?

    a. Matthew 21:21-22_____

    _____

    _____

    b. John 14:14 _____

c. John 15:16 _____

_____

_____

d. James 1:5-7_____

_____

_____

12. Where does God's power work, according to verse 20? What
kinds of things does that suggest to you that He might want to
do?

_____

_____

_____

_____

Apply what you have learned. Ephesians
3:21 concludes with a statement about God being
glorified in the church and in Christ Jesus *"throughout
all generations."* The church is made up of us and many other
people. Ephesians 2:7 makes it clear that God's purpose for
us is to *"show the immeasurable riches of His grace in kindness
toward us in Christ Jesus."* If we are personally aware of God's
kindness to us, we need to "show and tell." How have you
noticed God's kindness to you this week? Who can you tell
about it?

The Power and the Glory
Ephesians 3:14-21

Lost in Wonder, Love, and Praise (Ephesians 3:14-15)

After several digressions, Paul at last succeeds in penning the prayer that he intended in 3:l: *"For this reason I bow my knees before the Father"* (3:14). The mystery of God's will, the riches of his great love and mercy, the manifold wisdom of God—considering these indescribable gifts brings the apostle to his knees before God in praise and awe.

An Inner Knowledge as Big as Outer Space (Ephesians 3:16-19)

Paul reveals the content of his heartfelt prayer for the Ephesians. His desire for them is that, through the Holy Spirit, they have power to grasp the magnitude of God's love for them. He asks God to strengthen them *"with power ... in* [their] *inner being"* (3:16) *"so that Christ may dwell in* [their] *hearts through faith"* (3:17), and that they might be *"rooted and grounded"* in and *"comprehend"* (3:18) the love of Christ.

This prayer is similar to Paul's prayer in 1:18, that *"the eyes of your hearts* [may be] *enlightened."* Paul views knowledge and power as interrelated. The strength and power of 3:16 derive from *"His Spirit"* working in the *"inner being,"* allowing us to know Him. To know God is also to have His power. The Greek word for *knowledge, ginosko,* conveys a deep, intimate knowledge of another person. In general, it means a true knowledge derived from relationship rather than mere impersonal knowledge. Thus, in Ephesians 3:16 Paul speaks of the empowerment that comes from the Holy Spirit, who reveals God in ways that surpass human abilities to know Him.

>   **Think about** how, from a human viewpoint, there
> may be little visible difference in the attitudes or
> lifestyle of the person just beginning a walk toward
> God in Christ and the person walking away from
> God. But the ultimate destination of the first is eternal life
> and of the other eternal separation from God. Hence, the
> direction we are headed is very important, and sooner or
> later that direction will make an observable difference. We
> are people in process. Rather than measuring and criticizing
> one another's progress, why not concentrate on encouraging
> each other to go in the right direction and keeping our own
> course steady?

The Greek word for *dwell, katoikein,* means *establishing a permanent residence* as opposed to making an occasional visit. We receive Christ, and He dwells within our hearts, only through faith. In Colossians 1:27, Paul speaks of Christ's indwelling as the climax of the divine purpose: *"To them God chose to make known how great among the Gentiles are the riches of the glory of this mystery, which is Christ in you, the hope of glory."*

One consequence of Christ's indwelling is that the person becomes *"rooted and grounded in love"* (3:17). Paul prays that the Ephesians will *"have strength to comprehend with all the saints what is the breadth and length and height and depth, and to know the love of Christ"* (3:18). The Greek for *"may have strength"* implies a difficult task that calls for resolution and strength. The Greek word for *comprehend* is a military term that describes combat with a formidable opponent. In order to know Christ's love in all its magnitude, one must not be slack in pursuing that goal. This verse summons the reader to the front line on a battlefield.

Armies, rather than individuals, engage in battle. To know God is to know Him *"with all the saints."* Christian fellowship does not consist of solo artists performing individually. To know God requires an openness to learn from others, and a willingness to contribute to others. If God is greater than the peerless mysteries of the universe (*"How unsearchable are His judgments and how inscrutable His ways!"* Romans 11:33), then it would be foolish to think He can be fully comprehended with one sudden burst of energy or one short, intense period of discovery. He has called us and equipped us for something larger and longer, for a marathon of life.

Paul concludes his prayer with great boldness, *"that you may be filled with all the fullness of God"* (Ephesians 3:19). In Colossians 2:9, Paul says, *"In Him the whole fullness of deity dwells bodily."* Here, Paul boldly prays that Christ's followers will know God in His fullness. Paul has said *"we have boldness and access with confidence"* (Ephesians 3:12), and so he prays that *"we all attain ... to mature manhood, to the measure of the stature of the fullness of Christ"* (4:13).

Scripture clearly claims that God is actively involved in redeeming and restoring the universe. With this in mind, Paul uses the words *"filled"* and *"fullness"* (3:19). This is an audacious but appropriate prayer, for if Christ is the head of the church (1:22), then His fullness must also become its members' fullness. If Christ is Lord, then His nature must become the nature of those who follow Him. If the world is now disfigured, then awareness must grow that, in Christ's resurrection, God has begun the work of making all things new. Christ's return will signal the completion of that work and the ultimate answer to Paul's prayer.

A Doxology (Ephesians 3:20-21)

Paul concludes the first half of Ephesians with a *doxology (praise)* in 3:20-21. Normally, such doxologies occur at the end of his letters. In Ephesians, however, the break between the doctrinal (chapters 1-3) and the ethical sections (chapters 4-6) is more pronounced than in other Pauline letters.

Lest it seem Paul presumed too much in his prayer (Ephesians 3:14-19), he assures us in the doxology that God *"is able to do far more abundantly than all that we ask or think"* (3:20). Paul had a big God and was not ashamed to ask big things of Him.

This mighty and merciful God is worthy of *"glory in the church and in Christ Jesus"* (3:21). Paul calls the church the body of Christ and Christ the head of the church. Paul must therefore mean that God should be glorified in the church and in Jesus Christ. The church appears here on the same plane with Christ, a reminder to believers of their status and responsibility.

Personalize this lesson.

Do you believe that God can do all and more than you dare ask of Him? Consider the things you are praying about. Do you anticipate that God will answer *"far more abundantly"* than you ask or think? Ask Him to increase your faith so that your prayer requests give Him this opportunity to do the amazing and powerful things He wants to do—through you and to His glory!

Growing Into Christ's Likeness
Ephesians 4:1-16

Memorize God's Word: Ephesians 4:1.

❖ Ephesians 4:1-3—Living Worthy of Our Calling

1. Read Ephesians 4:1-6 and 3:1. What does Paul's statement that he is a *"prisoner for the Lord"* contribute to your understanding of this paragraph?

   _____

   _____

   _____

2. What significance do you see in Paul's instruction to *"maintain the unity"* rather than saying "work to *create* unity"?

   _____

   _____

   _____

   _____

❖ Ephesians 4:4-10—Unity in Christ

3. List the seven aspects of unity for believers.

   _____

   _____

   _____

   _____

4. Seven times the word *one* is used in these verses. What does this emphasis suggest to you?

_____

_____

_____

5. In the New Living Translation, Ephesians 4:7 is rendered, *"He has given each one of us a special gift through the generosity of Christ."* Read Romans 12:4-5 and explain in your own words why all our gifts are important.

_____

_____

_____

6. What specific gift did Jesus give when He ascended into heaven? (See John 14:16-17, Acts 1:3-9.)

_____

_____

_____

❖ Ephesians 4:11-13—Walking in Spiritual Gifts

7. Use the lists of spiritual gifts found in Ephesians 4:11-13; Romans 12:6-8; and 1 Corinthians 12:7-11 to make a compilation of the gifts.

_____

_____

_____

_____

8. Read also 1 Peter 4:10-11. For what reasons did God give spiritual gifts to the church?

_____

_____

_____

9. What gifts has God given you, and how are you using them?

_____

_____

_____

_____

❖ Ephesians 4:14-16—Growing in Maturity

10. a. How is *Christian maturity* described in 4:13? _____

_____

_____

   b. How is *spiritual infancy* described in verse 14? _____

_____

_____

11. Infants are inquisitive but not discerning, easily excited and easily exhausted, etc. What are some dangers that threaten a spiritual infant?

_____

_____

_____

12. How do you think *"speaking the truth in love"* could help us *"grow up in every way into Him* [Christ]*"*?

_____

_____

_____

13. How might a culture of *tolerance* keep us from *"speaking the truth in love"*? Explain your answer.

_____

_____

_____

_____

14. Give an example you have seen of a believer *"building another up"* in love.

_____

_____

_____

_____

15. Have you seen Christians try to "build each other up" without love? How could such situations be handled better?

_____

_____

_____

_____

Apply what you have learned. Paul is concerned that there be unity among the believers. Unity does not just happen. It must be worked at— or as Paul says, diligently kept (4:3). Mature believers will accentuate the things that preserve our God-given unity rather than the things that promote division (4:4-6). They will live godly lives (4:1-3) and use their giftedness to build up the body rather than to build up themselves (4:11-13). Do you feel that you are *"grow*[ing] *up"* (4:15)? You will be happier and the body will be healthier if you are doing what God has gifted you and called you to do—*"in love"*!

Growing Into Christ's Likeness
Ephesians 4:1-16

Unity in Christ (Ephesians 4:1-6)

Paul, again identifying himself as *"a prisoner for the Lord"* (4:1), is not ashamed of his chains. He considers them a badge of honor because they demonstrate his commitment to Christ. He has paid for the right to be heard and boldly urges his readers *"to walk in a manner worthy of the calling to which you have been called."*

The chief characteristics of a life *"worthy of the calling"* are humility, gentleness, patience, and bearing with one another in love (4:2). The Greek word for *bearing with* means *to endure or to put up with*. Like a muscle that must be exercised to become strong, *"bearing with one another in love"* thrives on a good workout. Not until we are challenged to love the unlovable, to bear with one who tries our patience, can Christian character be built and strengthened. It might be said that difficult relationships or situations are the essential ingredient God uses to build His children's character.

Another characteristic of a worthy life is *"maintain[ing] the unity of the Spirit"* (4:3). Paul does not say we must bring about unity. The unity of Christ's body is a gift of the Spirit that must be kept—maintained rather than attained. No unity is possible without *"the bond of peace."* Paul lists seven aspects of unity that believers hold in common, each prefaced with an emphatic *"one."* There is one body, one Spirit, one hope, one Lord, one faith, one baptism, one God and Father of us all.

One body refers to the church, and one Spirit to the Holy Spirit. The one hope is Christ. One Lord refers to Jesus Christ. One faith is the one means of salvation for all. Most theologians hold that one baptism refers to spiritual baptism and regeneration through the work of the Holy

Spirit. One God and Father recalls Israel's ancient creed, *"Hear, O Israel: The LORD our God, the LORD is one"* (Deuteronomy 6:4). Paul saw the unity of the world in Christ, a true unity consisting of the most diverse parts (see Colossians 3:11).

Becoming More Christ-like (Ephesians 4:7-16)

The means God has ordained to achieve unity are the *complementary gifts* Christ has given to each member of the body. This unity is not achieved by conformity or uniformity, but is fashioned from diversity. *"Grace was given to each one of us according to the measure of Christ's gift"* (4:7). This verse seems to imply various gifts of ministry to various individuals. Paul makes no distinctions of superiority—God has gifted each believer for the benefit of the whole.

Before developing this thought Paul takes a detour in 4:8-10—verses that are open to various interpretations. He quotes Psalm 68:18 and follows that with two verses about ascending and descending (Ephesians 4:9-10). What does he mean? Psalm 68 is a victory hymn composed by David and refers to a conquering king or general leading a procession of defeated captives up the holy hill (probably Mount Zion), having first received "gifts" or spoils of battle from them. However, there is an important difference. The psalm speaks of the king *receiving* gifts from men, whereas Paul speaks of the Messiah *giving* gifts to men. The ascended Christ gives gifts to His people for building the church. The point seems to be that Christ is the victorious king who has captured hostile forces, subjected them to His heavenly throne, and earned the right to distribute gifts to His subjects.

The enthroned Christ gives *apostles, prophets, evangelists, pastors and teachers* to the church. What is remarkable about this list is that Christ's gifts to the church come in the form of *gifted persons* whose job is to build the church and contribute to its development. The *one* grace (4:7) has *many* expressions and ministries. These specific gifts are given *"for building up the body of Christ"* for ministry. It is the people, not pastors and teachers, who are the ministers. The role of "professional" ministers is to equip and prepare *the people* to minister!

Verse 4:13 begins, *"until we all attain."* What is the goal? People from all different backgrounds come together as they grow in understanding the truth, learn to rely on the one Lord, and appreciate the concept of all being part of His one body. They *"become mature"* in order to *"attain … to the measure of the stature of the fullness of Christ."* When a person is "in Christ," he is destined to become like Him. Infant Christians can be easily influenced: *"children, tossed to and fro by the waves, and carried about by every wind of doctrine, by human cunning, by craftiness in deceitful schemes"* (4:14). Paul warns against the dangers of heresy and false teaching to which untaught, immature believers are especially susceptible.

In 4:14, Paul illustrates his warning with two images. *"Tossed to and fro by the waves, and carried about by every wind of doctrine"* recalls little boats on big seas, buffeted and foundering. The second image, *"cunning … craftiness … schemes,"* brings to mind business deals where subterfuge and trickery occur. The images are sobering. But they are not the last word.

Paul presents an inspiring contrast to the confusion and immaturity he has just described: *"Speaking the truth in love, we are to grow up"* (4:15-16). Truth and love—these are the most important characteristics of Christian maturity, the ones upon which all growth depends. Neither truth nor love, important as each is, can stand alone. Truth without love is harsh and potentially damaging, and love without truth is soft and sweet but without real substance. The purpose of truth and love is to *"grow up … into Him* [Christ]*"* (4:15). The goal of life is not to be your best self, but to be like Christ. He is *"your life"*—both its source and goal.

On a final note, passivity hinders the body's effective functioning. Each member must function actively if the body is to be healthy: *"We are to grow up in every way into Him"* by making godly choices.

Personalize this lesson.

The theme of this passage is that we are meant to fit together into a harmonious whole and, in the process, to reach Christian maturity. We are growing toward that maturity but have not yet reached it wholly, so it should come as no surprise that the church is not perfect. However, God is working in and through His imperfect church to accomplish His eternal purposes. He displays His grace in the lives of His people, for His Spirit is in us and working through us. How are you allowing God's grace to flow from you to the rest of the body? What contribution can you make to help the church become fully functional?

Lesson 9

Put off the Old Self, Put on the New
Ephesians 4:17-32

❖ **Ephesians 4:17-19—The Futility of Gentile Thinking**

1. Paul uses the term *Gentiles* here to describe nonbelievers even though he is writing to Gentiles who have come to Christ. How does Paul describe those who are futile in their thinking?

   _____

   _____

   _____

2. Some people are ignorant of God's love because they have never heard the gospel. Ephesians 4:18 tells us others are ignorant for another reason. Explain why in your own words.

   _____

   _____

   _____

3. Although Christ-followers are never separated from the life of God, they can still succumb to futile thinking. Give an example of such "futile thinking" and from Romans 12:2, suggest a way to safeguard against such thinking.

   _____

   _____

   _____

❖ Ephesians 4:20-27—Paul Contrasts the Believer's and Gentile's Mindset and Behavior

4. What are some of the characteristics of the *"old self"* that we must put off? (See also Colossians 3:5-11.)

    _____

    _____

    _____

5. What does Ephesians 4:22 say about assuming personal responsibility for our behavior?

    _____

    _____

    _____

6. How can unresolved anger give the devil a foothold in your life?

    _____

    _____

    _____

7. What kind of behavior will help keep anger from becoming a destructive force that destroys unity? (See Proverbs 15:1, 18; Hebrews 12:15.)

    _____

    _____

    _____

    _____

❖ Ephesians 4:28-30—Paul Continues His Exhortation

8. What does 4:28 give as a reason a person should be employed?

    _____

    _____

    _____

9. Fill in this chart with some of the advice from 4:25-32.

Do Not:	Do:	Reason For or Result of Such Behavior

10. Why is corrupting talk particularly displeasing to the Holy Spirit? (See also Ephesians 1:13-14; James 3:2-6.)

_____

_____

❖ Ephesians 4:31-32—Paul Explains How to Please the Holy Spirit

11. Verse 4:31 lists sins that grieve the Holy Spirit. Write a definition for each one below:

a. *bitterness* _____

_____

b. *wrath* _____

_____

c. *anger* _____

_____

d. *clamor* _____

_____

e. *slander* _____

_____

f. *malice* _____

_____

12. Verse 4:32 gives more positive instruction. Write a definition of

    a. *kind* _____

    _____

    b. *tenderhearted* _____

    _____

13. What is the standard by which we measure our level of forgiveness of others?

    _____

    _____

    _____

    _____

Apply what you have learned. Our "new self" has been created to be like God, and we are *"predestined ... to the praise of His glory"* (1:11-12). But how can we praise and glorify Him when we still lose our temper at the drop of a hat? Or when we are known as a liar? Or when we tell off-color jokes and make sexist or prejudicial remarks? What do you need to change? Ask God for wisdom and courage and strength to proceed.

Put off the Old Self, Put on the New
Ephesians 4:17-32

Putting on a New Person (Ephesians 4:17-24)

What, specifically, does it mean *"to walk in a manner worthy of the calling to which you have been called"*? (4:1). This is what Paul addresses now. *"Now this I say and testify in the Lord,"* begins Paul. *"No longer walk as the Gentiles do, in the futility of their minds ... darkened in their understanding"* (4:17-18). The Ephesians *were* Gentiles who had become Christians. In urging them to *"no longer walk as the Gentiles do,"* Paul exhorts that they not behave as they did before their conversion, though their former behavior was fully acceptable to the Gentile world. The change Paul speaks of runs deep, so he appeals to the mind and understanding (4:17-18). A worldly mindset results in a fundamentally wrong way of seeing self, others, the world, and God.

Paul's exposure of the unconverted understanding is thorough. He speaks of its futility—its emptiness, frustration, and lack of true purpose. He speaks of it being darkened, the exact opposite of the enlightened inner self he prayed for in Ephesians 1:18. *"Ignorance"* (4:18) is a serious matter. The ignorance Paul speaks of here is the consequence of a hardened heart, not a lack of education. A rare word in the New Testament, *porosis*, translated as *"hardness,"* means *numbness* or *deadness*. Becoming morally *"callous"* leads to depravity, *"to sensuality, greedy to practice every kind of impurity"* (4:19).

 Think about how believers are not in danger of the spiritual hardness that leads to eternal death, but we must, nevertheless, be careful not to flirt with sin, for the strength of its magnetic field seems to increase with exposure to it. And believers can be affected. The writer to the Hebrews warned, *"Take care, brothers, lest there be in any of you an evil, unbelieving heart, leading you to fall away from the living God. But exhort one another every day, as long as it is called 'today,' that none of you may be hardened by the deceitfulness of sin"* (Hebrews 3:12-13).

Paul states, *"But that is not the way you learned Christ!"* (Ephesians 4:20). It is somewhat unnatural to speak of "learning a person," but Paul's wording intends to refute heresies and false teachings (see 4:14). The idea seems to be *to learn the truth about Christ,* or *to be schooled in Christ.*

In 4:22-24, Paul uses the illustration of taking off and putting on clothes. Defining the Ephesians' former thinking and conduct as the *"old self,"* Paul orders them to strip it off and *"put on the new self, created after the likeness of God in true righteousness and holiness."* He sharpens this image by using three infinitives. *To put off* means a once-and-for-all act, to say good-bye forever to the past pattern of behavior. The second infinitive, *to be made new,* is in the present tense and means *to keep at it,* to commit oneself to the ongoing task of renewal. The final infinitive, *to put on,* means to make a final, resolute decision *to put on the new self.*

That the *"old self"* is dead is the true view of a believer's life, because it is God's view! If each believer is truly a new creature in God's eyes, we then have a responsibility to act in ways that are consistent with that truth. We need not worry that some residue from the past still lingers, for we *"are being transformed"* into His image (2 Corinthians 3:18)—and almighty God is helping us in the process. The point is to get started, right now, *"to put on the new self, created after the likeness of God in true righteousness and holiness"* (Ephesians 4:24).

What, Why, and Wherefore (Ephesians 4:25-32)

Paul focuses on six sins that characterize the *"old self"* and six virtues of the *"new self."* He follows a pattern: first a *prohibition,* then a *commandment,* and finally the reason for both. Paul begins with a commandment *against* falsehood and *for* truthfulness. Falsehood is a sin against trust, upon which all civilization and society, including the society of believers, is built. Turning to the emotion of *anger*, Paul quotes Psalm 4:4: *"Be angry, and do not sin."* The implication is that there is anger that is not sinful.

In Ephesians 4:28, the negative is *stealing* and the positive is *"honest work."* Stealing, of course, is wrong because it unjustly deprives others of their property. But that is not the only reason Paul condemns it. He urges us to *"labor, doing honest work,"* so we *"have something to share with anyone in need."* Paul implies that honest work enables generosity.

In 4:29-30, the negative is *"corrupting talk,"* and the positive is speech that *"is good for building up."* The Greek word for *corrupt, sapros,* means *rotten, worthless,* or *lifeless.* Paul is not denouncing obscenity or profanity only, but any speech that fails to build up its hearers. The purpose of language is *"for building up ... those who hear."* Paul's point is not simply that certain words are unbecoming or offensive; language that fails to edify *"grieve*[s] *the Holy Spirit of God."*

In 4:31, the listed negatives—*"bitterness and wrath and anger and clamor and slander"*—are all attitudes revealed in forms of speech that grieve the Holy Spirit. The Bible is clear that *speaking* a sin gives it permanence and paves the way for doing it.

The Christian characteristics of Ephesians 4:32 are not merely personal virtues but qualities that produce healthy relationships and Christian fellowship: *"Be kind to one another, tenderhearted, forgiving one another."* These qualities do not come from ourselves; they are things that Jesus Christ has modeled *for* us, and that God has given *to* us. Only *"in Christ"* do we receive the desire, the ability, and the pattern to become *"imitators of God"* (5:1).

Personalize this lesson.

☑ Resentment and anger break the unity of the body. This brokenness has brought far too much disrepute upon the church and disarray into the families within it. But God is more than able to help us with our anger. He can help us get to the roots of anger—which are often unmet expectations—and heal those wounded places in our hearts so that disappointment, irritations, and even provocations no longer cause us to seethe or boil over. If you struggle with anger, consider asking God a few questions: Why does _____ cause me to get so angry? Do I hold an expectation about this situation that is not being met? (e.g. "Life should always be fair," "I always need to be in control," or "If I don't perform perfectly, bad things will happen.") What do You think about this expectation? Is there a more healthy expectation You'd like me to have about this? Wait on Him silently to allow Him to reveal things to your heart. Respond to whatever He shows you with confession and a request for healing and help. His power is greater than your anger, and He longs to help you!

Lesson 10

The Imitation of Christ
Ephesians 5:1-20

Memorize God's Word: Ephesians 5:1.

❖ Ephesians 5:1-2—Our Calling

1. What relationship do we have with God that should motivate us to imitate Him?

    _____

    _____

    _____

2. In what ways can a human imitate God? Give specific examples from your own life.

    _____

    _____

    _____

    _____

    _____

3. With the help of the following passages, describe how a person can *"walk in love."*

    a. John 15:9-13 _____

        _____

    b. 1 John 3:16-18 _____

        _____

❖ Ephesians 5:3-7—Unacceptable Behavior

4. Why are Christians held to such a high moral standard, according to the following passages?

     a. Ephesians 1:4 _____

     _____

     b. 1 Thessalonians 4:3-7 _____

     _____

     c. 1 Peter 1:14-16 _____

     _____

5. a. One of the best tests of a holy life is the use of the tongue (James 3:2). What is your understanding of the examples of unholy speech given in Ephesians 5:4?

     1) *filthiness* _____

     2) *foolish talk* _____

     3) *crude joking* _____

     b. What does Ephesians 5:4 say is the alternative to such talk?

     _____

     _____

❖ Ephesians 5:8-14—Children of Light

6. List some characteristics of physical darkness.

     _____

     _____

     _____

     _____

7. What insight into understanding spiritual darkness does your list give you?

     _____

     _____

     _____

8. List some characteristics of physical light.

_____

_____

_____

9. What insight into understanding spiritual light does the list you created in question 8 give you?

_____

_____

10. What do Psalm 1:1-2 and John 8:31-32 tell you about how to *"discern what is pleasing to the Lord"* (Ephesians 5:10)?

_____

_____

11. According to 5:11, what are two ways a Christian should respond to *"works of darkness"*?

_____

_____

_____

❖ Ephesians 5:15-20—Walking Wisely

12. According to 5:15-17, we need to be wise and make the most of our opportunities. What do you understand this to mean?

_____

_____

_____

13. *Wisdom* might be defined as *viewing life from God's perspective.* How does it differ from

a. *intelligence?* _____

_____

_____

b. *knowledge?* _____

    _____

    _____

14. "Beautiful music … is one of the most magnificent and delightful presents God has given us" (Martin Luther). Why do you think music is important in a Christian's life and worship?

    _____

    _____

15. Why should we thank God *"always and for everything"*? (See Ephesians 5:20; Romans 8:28; 1 Thessalonians 5:18.)

    _____

    _____

Apply what you have learned. To live a life filled with love, to avoid being deceived, to walk in light not darkness, to be wise and always be thankful—what a challenge Paul issues to the believers at Ephesus! And what a challenge for us today! As you think about these potential growth areas, is there one that seems most relevant to where you are today? Ask God to help you—and thank Him for His Holy Spirit who fills us and empowers us to live a God-blessed life.

Lesson 10 Commentary

The Imitation of Christ
Ephesians 5:1-20

Imitating God (Ephesians 5:1-20)

This thought-provoking idea of imitating God is present everywhere in the Bible. The Old Testament repeatedly describes God as holy, true, just, and merciful, while at the same time demanding these qualities of those who worship Him. "Imitating God" is to be understood in a moral sense: *"walk in love"* (5:2). The source of selfless conduct is Christ Himself, who *"loved us and gave Himself up for us."*

A *"fragrant offering"* (5:2) may seem an odd expression. In the Old Testament, a sacrifice properly burned was said to be a pleasing aroma to God, who is pleased by Christ's sacrifice, not by good works. Our words and deeds please God only when they have *"the aroma of Christ"* (2 Corinthians 2:15).

Things That Have No Place in Christian Fellowship (Ephesians 5:3-7)

In chapter 4, Paul called for putting away falsehood, anger, stealing, unwholesome talk, bitterness, and other sins. But here he says these sins *"must not even be named among you"* (5:3).

The Greek word for *"sexual immorality,"* *porneia*, included every kind of unlawful sexual activity. *"Impurity,"* coupled with *porneia*, means any form of depraved sexual behavior. Paul's criterion is that such behavior is not *"proper among saints."* Paul adds, *"Let there be no filthiness nor foolish talk nor crude joking"* (5:4). The root for *filthy* is *ugly* or *wicked*. Both ideas are present here. The inclusion of *"foolish talk"* and *"crude joking"* may hit closer to home for many Christians.

Paul then calls for *"thanksgiving"* (5:4). Two things can be said of thanksgiving. First, *"filthiness ... foolish talk ... crude joking"* are all forms of degrading speech, whereas thanksgiving is the opposite; it honors God and builds up fellow believers. Thankfulness is a chief characteristic of Christians. Second, thanksgiving is probably the most effective antidote to idolatry. In 5:5, Paul says that the three sins of verse 3 lead ultimately to idolatry. An idolater is someone who has elevated something above God. Thanksgiving can keep God first and central.

Paul concludes: *"You may be sure of this, that everyone who is sexually immoral or impure, or who is covetous ... has no inheritance in the kingdom of Christ and God"* (5:5). Paul is not speaking of evildoers outside the church; the Bible is clear that anyone, no matter how wicked, can be saved if he or she turns to Christ. The problem is with those who have brought their old ways with them into the kingdom. They have not made a clean break with the past (2:1-3); they have not put off the old self (4:22-24). People who continue to sin repeatedly with no effort to repent reveal that they are trying to accommodate two incompatible worlds. As a result of not truly giving up the old, they cannot inherit the new. Something in the old is still more important to the *"idolater"* than *"the kingdom of Christ and God."*

"Let no one deceive you with empty words" (5:6), Paul says. He is surely cautioning against the influence of people who make light of—perhaps even affirm—conduct that is absolutely unacceptable to God and totally inappropriate for any of God's people. There must be no compromise with immorality. God's wrath makes no peace with unrighteousness: *"Do not become partners with them"* (5:7).

Think about how all of us, Christian or not, are exposed to and acquire values and attitudes that are profoundly non-Christian. Our challenge is to be *"in the world"* but *"not of the world"* (John 17:14-18)—a difficult balance to achieve. That is why Paul wrote, *"Do not be conformed to this world, but be transformed by the renewal of your mind"* (Romans 12:2). *"Renewal"* is a process that, in our hedonistic culture, requires continual cleansing. God's Word cleanses like a powerful detergent. It enlightens like a bright spotlight so we can "see" the places where the world has left dark stains on our value system and influenced our behavior. If we study the Word, the reward is worth our best efforts.

Light That Transforms Darkness (Ephesians 5:8-14)

Of the Gentiles, Paul says, *"At one time you were darkness, but now you are light in the Lord"* (5:8). Believers are light only because Christ is light and they are *"in Christ."* This makes us *"light in the Lord,"* children *"of light,"* yielding *"the fruit of light,"* which is *"all that is good and right and true"* (5:9). Fruit is not a work, but a natural outgrowth. In the same way, goodness, righteousness, and truth are not works, but the natural result of Christ's life in us. The presence of His light enables believers to *"discern what is pleasing to the Lord"* (5:10). We are told to *"take no part in the unfruitful works of darkness."* Instead of participating in *"unfruitful works,"* believers are to *"expose"* them. Light makes things formerly hidden *"visible"* (5:13); and it not only exposes darkness, it transforms it!

Walking in Wisdom (Ephesians 5:15-17)

For the fifth time, Paul exhorts the Ephesians to *"look carefully then how you walk"* (5:15). The Christian walk demands that believers live *"not as unwise but as wise."* The wise are careful and caring. They *"mak[e] the best use of the time"* (5:16). All time and circumstances, no matter how unfortunate or evil they may be, afford opportunities for love and service. Seize them and allow Christ to transform them for redemptive purposes. Be aware of the possibilities around you and *"understand what the will of the Lord is"* (5:17).

A Life of Praise (Ephesians 5:18-20)

Paul begins this section with a command against drunkenness and makes a play on words: Instead of being filled with alcohol, be filled with the Spirit.

Paul gives five different ways to express praise: *"psalms,"* *"hymns,"* and *"spiritual songs,"* to *"sing,"* and *"mak[e] melody ... with your heart"* (5:19). In the early church, the rigid legalism of Pharisaic Judaism and the anxiety and fatalism of paganism had melted before the unspeakable joy of abundant life in Jesus Christ. Giving thanks is something to be done *"always and for everything."*

Personalize this lesson.

Like perfume permeates the air, the character of Christ should permeate our lives, our minds, our attitudes, our actions. That "fragrance" should be so obvious that others notice it. How do you spread the aroma of Christ in your family, workplace, or church? Is it through your servant heart? Your peaceful spirit? Your honesty and integrity? Ask God to make you even more fragrant so that through you, He can "[spread] *the fragrance of the knowledge of Him everywhere*" (2 Corinthians 2:14).

Lesson 11

Divine Rules for Human Relationships
Ephesians 5:21–6:9

❖ **Ephesians 5:21—Paul Urges Mutual Submission**

1. According to this verse, how does our attitude toward Christ influence our submission to people? (See also 5:1-2; Philippians 2:3-7.)

_____

_____

_____

2. How might applying 5:21 impact and significantly change one of your relationships?

_____

_____

_____

❖ **Ephesians 5:22-24—The Relationship of Wives to Husbands Is Addressed**

3. What is the connection between a wife's relationship with Christ and her relationship with her husband?

_____

_____

_____

_____

4. Because Christ is held out as the example in this passage, it should be helpful to examine how submission worked in His life.

   a. According to the following passages, did Christ submit to the Father?

      1) Matthew 26:36-39 _____

      2) John 4:31-34 _____

   b. According to the following passages, is Christ inferior to the Father?

      1) John 1:1-3, 18 _____

      2) Colossians 1:15-20 _____

❖ Ephesians 5:25-33—Paul Addresses Husbands

5. From these verses, how would you describe the kind of love Christ has for the church?

   _____

   _____

   _____

6. Based on what you understand from this passage, how does God expect husbands to love their wives? Suggest some specific ways they could do this.

   _____

   _____

   _____

   _____

7. What does Paul tell wives to do in verse 33? Contrast this with what he instructed in verse 22. How are these two instructions similar? How are they different?

   _____

   _____

   _____

   _____

8. Why do you suppose Paul told husbands to love their wives, but told wives to submit to and respect their husbands?

_____

_____

❖ Ephesians 6:1-4—Paul Addresses Parents and Children

9. According to the following verses, what are some reasons Paul may have had for urging children to obey?

a. Proverbs 6:20-23 _____

_____

b. Ephesians 6:3 _____

_____

10. What moderating influence should 6:4 have on a parent who is tempted to be overly strict, overbearing, arbitrary, or harsh?

_____

_____

11. What character traits of God as heavenly Father could help prevent parents from provoking their children to anger? (See Psalm 103:8, 13-14; 1 John 2:6.)

_____

_____

❖ Ephesians 6:5-9—Suggestions for Conduct and Attitude in the Workplace

NOTE: Although the specific relationship addressed is master and slave, the principles given are applicable to employer and employee.

12. According to the following passages, what should be the attitude of a Christian employee toward his or her employer?

a. Ephesians 6:5-6 _____

_____

b.   1 Peter 2:18-19 _____

_____

13. Put into your own words the instructions Paul gave the Ephesian employers and masters and comment on their relevance today.

_____

_____

_____

_____

14. The command for children to obey their parents is restricted by the phrase *"in the Lord"* (6:1). Are there times when children (and wives, employees, citizens, etc.) should not submit to those in authority? What scriptures might support your answer?

_____

_____

_____

_____

Apply what you have learned. When Paul wrote this letter, wives, children, and slaves had no recognized legal or human rights. Yet he exhorted the Ephesian believers to value reciprocity and respect in relationships. If Christ is to be honored and His people are to contribute to the stability of the social and economic structure of their culture in any century, this mutual give-and-take must be tempered by a mutual reverence for Christ and a respect for each other. Who do you regularly interact with who holds a subordinate position to you? Your children? Your employees? How can you demonstrate respect to these people and communicate to them their value to both you and to God?

Divine Rules for Human Relationships
Ephesians 5:21–6:9

Life for Others (Ephesians 5:21)

Paul states a single, powerful principle: *"Submit to one another out of reverence for Christ"* (5:21, NIV). He then applies this principle to three basic relationships: marriage, family, and employment. The motive for submission is *"reverence for Christ."* This is not a slavish, cowering fear, but a reverential awe that a believer might sense in God's presence.

Wives (Ephesians 5:22-33)

A wife is to submit to her husband because he is her *"head"* (5:23). The church recognizes and honors Christ as the head; similarly, the wife is to honor her husband's headship (5:24). Paul is speaking about roles, not about worth. He is not saying men are superior. Nor does he teach the subordination of women to just any man—he is addressing wives and their husbands. The wife's responsibility to submit is defined by the phrase *"as to the Lord"* (5:22). Christ treats the church as His body and rules the church in a way that facilitates growth and perfection. Christ neither takes advantage of nor misguides the church into unholy purposes. *"As to the Lord"* thus determines that submission is an act of self-giving to a husband whose love is sacrificial.

Husbands (Ephesians 5:25-33)

Paul then moves from the issue of headship to love. *"Husbands, love your wives"* (5:25). The harder command is to love one's wife *"as Christ loved the church and gave Himself up for her."* Sacrifice is the very nature of Christ's love. This love is not an unattainable ideal that discourages and defeats. Christ, who died for the church, empowers husbands with His love. Christ's ministry to the church is to make her holy, cleanse her, and present her to Himself. *"The washing of water with the word"* (5:26) likely refers to the Word of God as the agent of purification. The condition of the church when presented to Christ is described as *"without spot or wrinkle or any such thing ... holy and without blemish"* (Ephesians 5:27).

Husbands should also *"love their wives as their own bodies"* (5:28). The goal of marriage is that two become one in a mysterious and profound relationship. The love of the other, therefore, is also the love of self. Thus, *"He who loves his wife loves himself."* This is common sense: *"For no one ever hated his own flesh, but nourishes and cherishes it"* (5:29). As Christ nourishes and cherishes the church, so should husbands seek ways to encourage their wives to live holy and blameless lives. The marriage union is God's plan for a deep, trusting, lasting relationship—a special unity designed at Creation. That is the reason for quoting Genesis 2:24 in Ephesians 5:31. The emphasis falls on *"the two shall become one flesh."* When, in mutual submission and love, two people join together in marriage, two become one.

Children (Ephesians 6:1-3)

The apostle's word to children begins, *"Obey your parents in the Lord"* (6:1). Paul gives four reasons for this command. First, their obedience is to be comparable to their obedience to Christ. It could be said that in learning to obey parents they learn to obey God. The second is that it is *"right,"* approved by God. Third, the Fifth Commandment (Exodus 20:12) calls for it. Finally, they are given a promise of blessing if they do so.

Parents (Ephesians 6:4)

This verse is addressed to *"Fathers,"* but it applies to both parents because children are enjoined to obey their *"parents"* (6:1). Paul designates four characteristics of a father's authority. First is a command not to *"provoke your children to anger."* The idea is not to discipline a child in a manner that will result in resentment or a simmering sense of injustice. Authority can be used to break a child's spirit, but a wise parent trains a child in a way that leads to trust and maturity. Second, fathers are commanded to *"bring ... up"* their children, which carries the sense of *nourishing* and *cherishing*. The third command, *"discipline,"* includes *teaching* and *discipline*. Finally, fathers are charged with the *"instruction"* of their children. This word contains the sense of *warning admonition* and instructs parents to be clear about boundaries and the consequences of trespassing them.

Most importantly, Paul designates that parents should give their children *"instruction of the Lord"* (6:4).

Think about the enormous responsibility of parents. Children tend to follow patterns they see daily, even when they are bad patterns. For example, children who have been abused often become abusers themselves. Every parent makes mistakes. But good parents apologize when they do. Never be afraid to say to your child, "I'm sorry" or "I was wrong. Will you forgive me?" If your child knows you love him or her, that love will compensate for many of the mistakes you make. So talk to your children. Talk also to God. Take all your concerns and failures to the Lord in prayer. Ask His forgiveness and ask for wisdom and strength to be the kind of parent your children need.

Slaves (Ephesians 6:5-8)

As Rome conquered nations, it took able-bodied men and women into slavery. Paul's exhortation to *"bondservants"* to obey their masters does not imply that he approved of slavery—he did not. He wrote to slaves and masters not to condone slavery but to try, by Christ's teachings, to humanize it. Slaves' masters are only *"earthly masters"* (6:5); nevertheless, slaves should serve them not because of external compulsion, but *"with a sincere heart."* Behind Paul's thought is the idea that whatever a believer does for others (even unjust others), he does for Christ. This teaching presents two important lessons: Christians can experience freedom within human bondage, and Christians are servants of Christ.

Masters (Ephesians 6:9)

Masters are to desist from threats and not show favoritism. They are to treat those in their charge with fairness. The condition of their servants is to remind them that they, too, have a Master to whom they are responsible. This truth is still valid for anyone who holds a position of authority over others.

Personalize this lesson.

☑ All our relationships have eternal significance. They are the vehicles by which we express our love for Christ and in which we are blessed. Even difficult relationships that are travesties of what God intended are not beyond redemption. The Christian's responsibility is to be God's person in every situation. *"Put on then, as God's chosen ones, holy and beloved, compassionate hearts, kindness, humility, meekness, and patience"* (Colossians 3:12). Sometimes the most difficult relationships provide the greatest opportunity to experience intimacy with Christ and grow in His character. Are you in a difficult relationship? Or do you know someone who is? How could greater compassion, kindness, humility, meekness, or patience be a step toward healing in this relationship? Ask God to change hearts (yours or the person's you are praying for) so that this healing can begin.

Lesson 12

The Armor of God
Ephesians 6:10-24

Memorize God's Word: Ephesians 6:10-11.

❖ **Ephesians 6:10-12—The Christian's Strength and Struggle**

1. According to the following verses, what is the source of a believer's strength?

   a. Psalm 68:35 _____

   b. 1 John 4:4 _____

2. What is your responsibility in the spiritual battle, according to Ephesians 6:11? (See also 2 Corinthians 2:11.)

   _____

   _____

3. What does verse 6:12 say to those who think that all problems will disappear if they become Christians? Feel free to use your own experience in the discussion.

   _____

   _____

   _____

4. Who does Paul say the battle is against? Is *not* against? Why is this distinction so important?

   _____

   _____

5. Some people today deny the existence of the devil. But the Bible teaches us about the one called Satan, the accuser, the god of this age, the prince of the power of the air, etc. According to the following passages, what are some of Satan's objectives?

    a. Luke 8:5, 11-12 _____

       _____

       _____

    b. 2 Corinthians 4:3-4 _____

       _____

       _____

    c. 1 Peter 5:8-9 _____

       _____

       _____

❖ Ephesians 6:13-17—The Christian's Armor

6. What suggestions for handling Satan's attacks can you glean from the following verses?

    a. Matthew 4:1-11 _____

       _____

       _____

    b. James 4:7 _____

       _____

       _____

7. Consider the armor issued to each Christian for the spiritual battle.

In the first column of the chart on the next page, list each piece of armor and put a check beside each offensive weapon.

In the second column, record any insight you have about its significance.

List each piece and put a check beside each offensive weapon.	For deeper thought: Record any insight you have about its significance.
a.	
b.	
c.	
d.	
e.	
f.	

❖ Ephesians 6:18-20—The Christian's Battle

8. According to Ephesians 6:18, when should we pray?

   _____

   _____

9. How should we pray?

   _____

   _____

10. For whom should we pray?

    _____

    _____

11. From Ephesians 6:19-20, what two things did Paul most want his Christian friends to ask God to give him?

    _____

    _____

12. Read 2 Corinthians 5:20-21. What does it mean to be an
    "ambassador for Christ"?

    _____

    _____

    _____

❖ Ephesians 6:21-24—Paul's Conclusion

13. What do you learn about Paul's love for these believers?

    _____

    _____

14. Stop here and pray for someone you know who is having a very
    difficult time. Try to incorporate some of Paul's benediction
    (6:23-24) in your prayer.

    _____

    _____

    _____

    _____

    _____

Apply what you have learned. Paul warns the
Ephesians that they will encounter opposition from
"spiritual forces of evil." The devil will scheme to
take away their victory and steal their spiritual riches. The
warning is equally relevant today. We, too, need to put on
the full armor of God and take a stand. But *know* that *"the
battle is the LORD's"* even if you *feel* less than adequate. What
spiritual battle do you currently face? What stand is God
calling you to make and what armor does He invite you to
take up?

Lesson 12 Commentary

The Armor of God
Ephesians 6:10-24

The Spiritual Battle (Ephesians 6:10-13)

Paul makes a call to arms: *"Be strong in the Lord and in the strength of His might"* (6:10). *"Put on the whole armor of God,"* Paul commands (6:11). Believers are outfitted with God's invincible armor, which assures victory in the face of evil. The tone is urgent: enough of laziness, procrastination, self-doubt, polite excuses. There are still battles to be fought—the Ephesian Christians must snap to attention. To be a Christian is to join no ordinary battle. *"We do not wrestle against flesh and blood, but against the rulers, against the authorities, against the cosmic powers over this present darkness, against the spiritual forces of evil in the heavenly places"* (6:12). No Christian is excused from this battle.

The Armor of God (Ephesians 6:14-17)

Paul lists six pieces of equipment and their corresponding virtues: belt of truth, breastplate of righteousness, feet shod for peace, shield of faith, helmet of salvation, and sword of the Word. Soldiers in Paul's time wore a leather belt to keep their clothes tight against their body, to lessen the chance that an enemy might be able to seize the loose garment. Shields, breastplates, and helmets were constructed to withstand various types of assault. The imagery suggests that this armor is helpful only if the believer stands and faces evil.

Next, notice the footgear. When Paul mentions *"shoes for your feet ... the readiness given by the gospel of peace,"* he may be recalling Isaiah 52:7. The peace that the believer proclaims, experiences, and defends is the peace of Christ. The only offensive weapon mentioned is *"the sword of the Spirit, which is the word of God"* (6:17). Scripture often refers to God's Word as a sword.

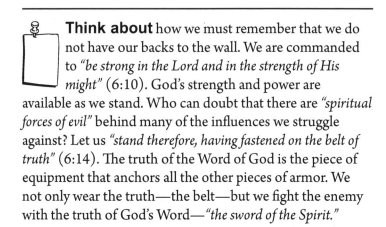

Think about how we must remember that we do not have our backs to the wall. We are commanded to *"be strong in the Lord and in the strength of His might"* (6:10). God's strength and power are available as we stand. Who can doubt that there are *"spiritual forces of evil"* behind many of the influences we struggle against? Let us *"stand therefore, having fastened on the belt of truth"* (6:14). The truth of the Word of God is the piece of equipment that anchors all the other pieces of armor. We not only wear the truth—the belt—but we fight the enemy with the truth of God's Word—*"the sword of the Spirit."*

The Prayerful Warrior (Ephesians 6:18-20)

Paul concludes his strategy with a rather unexpected turn that might seem odd to a military strategist: he speaks of *"praying at all times in the Spirit, with all prayer and supplication"* (6:18). He who combats evil must fall on his knees before God in prayer and entreaty, not trusting in his armor but in the Commander-in-Chief who provided it. Prayer and alertness are the first order for active duty.

In light of Paul's admonition to *"keep alert with all perseverance, making supplication for all the saints,"* he pleads, *"and also for me"* (6:19). No doubt, from time to time Paul's chains and confinement (6:20) tempted him to discouragement. Yet, even as a prisoner, Paul seeks to make *"the best use of the time"* (5:16). He requests that *"the words may be given to me in opening my mouth"* (6:19). This odd expression can only be a refrain of Psalm 51:15 or Ezekiel 3:27, where God opens His messenger's mouth and speaks through it. Paul may be in chains, but the gospel must not be chained. Twice he asks for prayer to enable him to speak *"boldly"* so that he, *"an ambassador in chains"* (6:20), may *"proclaim the mystery of the gospel"* (6:19).

Undying Love (Ephesians 6:21-24)

With these words, Paul brings this compelling epistle to a close. This is surely not the end of Paul's impact on believers. The Christian pilgrimage is like a good book that you do not want to put down. It is a never-ending story. For as long as the world endures, Christians will be attempting to live out the teachings of this book—to make the applications, to claim the power.

Tychicus, a native of Asia, delivered this letter. Probably a delegate from the Colossian church, he, along with Trophimus from Ephesus, accompanied Paul on his final trip to Jerusalem. Tychicus, it appears, remained with Paul through the better part of this unjust imprisonment.

The Ephesians might have expected a gloomy report about Paul, whose prospects had deteriorated further since he had, in all likelihood, been transferred to Rome. Yet it was anything but a hand-wringing condolence that the Ephesians received from Tychicus. *"I have sent him ... that he may encourage your hearts,"* writes Paul (6:22). The report that Tychicus brought surely included details of Paul's imprisonment, but its tone was certainly not determined by that news. Instead, *"peace ... love ... faith ... grace"* (6:23-24) are key words in his final greeting.

Ephesians ends unlike any other Pauline epistle. *"With love incorruptible"* (6:24) is Paul's closing word, *aphtharsia* in Greek, which means *indestructible, immortal. Aphtharsia* is the promise of something in the future, something determined by God. It is something glorious, imperishable, enduring. And so this epistle, which began with a bold glance to the eternal past, closes with a forward gaze at eternal hope.

In the first three chapters, Paul describes the incredible spiritual blessings that belong to us in Christ. In the final three chapters, he encourages believers to bring their lifestyle into alignment with the reality of those blessings—living changed and triumphant in the strength God provides. Although the book ends, the future is bright, for the future belongs to Christ, and we walk forward with confident hope.

Personalize this lesson.

 When this epistle was written, the Roman Empire, like a bad apple, was rotting from the core. Ephesus was one of the most influential cities in the empire—and one of the most decadent. The majority of citizens were intellectually proud and had adopted an "anything goes" attitude toward religion and sexuality. Paul seeks to emphasize truth and the logical response to it. He seems convinced that there are good Christian people in the city who need to be strengthened for their own sakes and "stirred up" for the sake of their nation. They can still make a difference in their crumbling societal structure if they grasp who they are *"in Christ"* and make the proper response to that knowledge. Sound familiar? How has this study stirred you to action? What specific plans will you make to follow through?

Small Group Leader's Guide

While *Engaging God's Word* is great for personal study, it is generally even more effective and enjoyable when studied with others. Studying with others provides different perspectives and insights, care, prayer support, and fellowship that studying on your own does not. Depending on your personal circumstances, consider studying with your family or spouse, with a friend, in a Sunday school, with a small group at church, work, or in your neighborhood, or in a mentoring relationship.

In a traditional Community Bible Study class, your study would involve a proven four-step method: personal study, a small group discussion facilitated by a trained leader, a lecture covering the passage of Scripture, and a written commentary about the same passage. *Engaging God's Word* provides two of these four steps with the study questions and commentary. When you study with a group, you add another of these—the group discussion. And if you enjoy teaching, you could even provide a modified form of the fourth, the lecture, which in a small group setting might be better termed a wrap-up talk.

Here are some suggestions to help leaders facilitate a successful group study.

1. Decide how long you would like each group meeting to last. For a very basic study, without teaching, time for fellowship, or group prayer, plan on one hour. If you want to allow for fellowship before the meeting starts, add at least 15 minutes. If you plan to give a short teaching, add 15 or 20 minutes. If you also want time for group prayer, add another 10 or 15 minutes. Depending on the components you include for your group, each session will generally last between one and two hours.

2. Set a regular time and place to meet. Meeting in a church classroom or a conference room at work is fine. Meeting in a home is also a good option, and sometimes more relaxed and comfortable.

3. Publicize the study and/or personally invite people to join you.

4. Begin praying for those who have committed to come. Continue to pray for them individually throughout the course of the study.

5. Make sure everyone has his or her own book at least a week before you meet for the first time.

6. Encourage group members to read the first lesson and do the questions before they come to the group meeting.

7. Prepare your own lesson.

8. Prepare your wrap-up talk, if you plan to give one. Here is a simple process for developing a wrap-up talk:

   a. Divide the passage you are studying into two or three divisions. Jot down the verses for each division and describe the content of each with one complete sentence that answers the question, "What is the passage about?"

   b. Decide on the central idea of your wrap-up talk. The central idea is the life-changing principle found in the passage that you believe God wants to implant in the hearts and minds of your group. The central idea answers the question, "What does God want us to learn from this passage?"

   c. Provide one illustration that would make your central idea clear and meaningful to your group. This could be an illustration from your own life, or a story you've read or heard somewhere else.

   d. Suggest one application that would help your group put the central idea into practice.

   e. Choose an aim for your wrap-up talk. The aim answers the question, "What does God want us to do about it?" It encourages specific change in your group's lives, if they choose to respond to the central idea of the passage. Often it takes the form of a question you will ask your group: "Will you, will I choose to … ?"

9. Show up early to the study so you can arrange the room, set up the refreshments (if you are serving any), and welcome people as they arrive.

10. Whether your meeting includes a fellowship time or not, begin the discussion time promptly each week. People appreciate it when you respect their time. Transition into the discussion with prayer, inviting God to guide the discussion time and minister personally to each person present.

11. Model enthusiasm to the group. Let them know how excited you are about what you are learning—and your eagerness to hear what God is teaching them.

12. As you lead through the questions, encourage everyone to participate, but don't force anyone. If one or two people tend to dominate the discussion, encourage quieter ones to participate by saying something like, "Let's hear from someone who hasn't shared yet." Resist the urge to teach during discussion time. This time is for your group to share what they have been discovering.

13. Try to allow time after the questions have been discussed to talk about the "Apply what you have learned," "Think about" and "Personalize this lesson" sections. Encourage your group members in their efforts to partner with God in allowing Him to transform their lives.

14. Transition into the wrap-up talk, if you are doing one (see number 8).

15. Close in prayer. If you have structured your group to allow time for prayer, invite group members to pray for themselves and one another, especially focusing on the areas of growth they would like to see in their lives as a result of their study. If you have not allowed time for group prayer, you as leader can close this time.

16. Before your group finishes their final lesson, start praying and planning for what your next *Engaging God's Word* study will be.

About Community Bible Study

For almost 40 years Community Bible Study
has taught the Word of God through in-depth,
community-based Bible studies. With nearly 700
classes in the United States as well as classes in
more than 70 countries, Community Bible Study purposes to be an
"every-person's Bible study, available to all."

Classes for men, women, youth, children, and even babies, are all
designed to make members feel loved, cared for, and accepted—
regardless of age, ethnicity, socio-economic status, education, or
church membership. Because Bible study is most effective in one's heart
language, Community Bible Study curriculum has been translated into
more than 50 languages.

Community Bible Study makes every effort to stand in the center of the
mainstream of historic Christianity, concentrating on the essentials of
the Christian faith rather than denominational distinctives. Community
Bible Study respects different theological views, preferring to focus on
helping people to know God through His Word, grow deeper in their
relationships with Jesus, and be transformed into His likeness.

Community Bible Study's focus ... is to glorify God by providing
in-depth Bible studies and curriculum in a Christ-centered, grace-filled,
and philosophically safe environment.

Community Bible Study's passion ... is the transformation of
individuals, families, communities, and generations through the power
of God's Word, making disciples of the Lord Jesus Christ.

Community Bible Study's relationship with local churches ... is one
of support and respect. Community Bible Study classes are composed of
people from many different churches; they are designed to complement
and not compete with the ministry of the local church. Recognizing that
the Lord has chosen the local church as His primary channel of ministry,
Community Bible Study encourages class members to belong to and
actively support their local churches and to be servants and leaders in
their congregations.

Do you want to experience lasting transformation in your life? Are you ready to go deeper in God's Word? There is probably a Community Bible Study near you! Find out by visiting www.findmyclass.org or scan the QR code on this page.

For more information:

Call   800-826-4181

Email   info@communitybiblestudy.org

Web   www.communitybiblestudy.org

Class   www.findmyclass.org

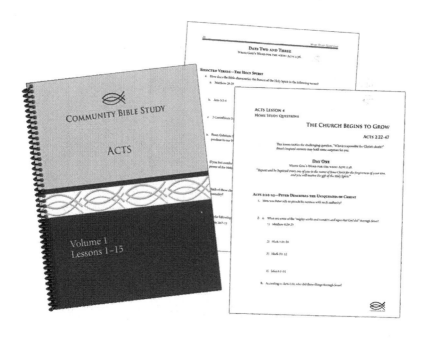

Where will your next Bible study adventure take you?

Engage Bible Studies help you discover the joy and the richness of God's Word and apply it your life.

Check out these titles for your next adventure:

Engaging God's Word: Genesis

Engaging God's Word: Deuteronomy

Engaging God's Word: Joshua & Judges

Engaging God's Word: Daniel

Engaging God's Word: Job

Engaging God's Word: Mark

Engaging God's Word: Luke

Engaging God's Word: Acts

Engaging God's Word: Romans

Engaging God's Word: Galatians

Engaging God's Word: Ephesians

Engaging God's Word: Philippians

Engaging God's Word: Colossians

Engaging God's Word: 1 & 2 Thessalonians

Engaging God's Word: Hebrews

Engaging God's Word: James

Engaging God's Word: 1 & 2 Peter

Engaging God's Word: Revelation

Available at Amazon.com and in fine bookstores.

Visit engagebiblestudies.com